Infant/Toddler

Introducing Your Child to the Joy of Learning

by Earladeen Badger, Ph.D.

Foreword by J. McVicker Hunt, Ph. D.

A PARENT/CAREGIVER BOOK

instructo™

INSTRUCTO/McGraw-Hill

Following conventional use of pronouns in early childhood literature and for the ease of reading, only one pronoun, the masculine form, has been used throughout this book.

Editor: Maureen H. Cook
Editorial Consultant: Martha Hochschwender

Illustrations: Renee Quintal Daily

Cover Design: Gil Lieberman
Typesetting: Rosanne McFadden

First printing June 1981
Second printing December 1981

Library of Congress Cataloging in Publication Data

Badger, Earladeen.
    Infant/toddler, introducing your child to the joy of learning.

    1. Child development—Problems, exercises, etc.
2. Play—Problems, exercises, etc.   3. Domestic education—
Problems, exercises, etc.   4. Infants.
I. Title.
HQ769.B26   649'.68   81-8263
ISBN 0-07-530334-5   AACR2

Printed in the United States of America
10 9 8 7 6 5 4 3

Preface

The notion of involving mothers as teachers in a sequenced educational program for their young children began with my work in a research program at the Urbana Campus of the University of Illinois. The intelligence gains shown by these children and the enthusiastic endorsement of their mothers who participated in a two-year pilot program validated the idea of mother-as-teacher as well as the use of a highly specific curriculum during the infant-toddler years.[1]

Since a low budget was possible when mothers served as teachers, it proved feasible with the federal funding of Parent Child Centers to extend this program beyond the research setting. The Mothers' Training Program in conjunction with the experimental edition of the *Infant/Toddler Learning (ITL) Program* have been field-tested with highly encouraging results in Parent Child Centers in Mt. Carmel, Illinois, and Chattooga County, Georgia,[2] in an orphanage in Teheran,[3] and in the Newborn Division of University of Cincinnati College of Medicine.[4] Further, the favorable response received from hundreds of professionals in early childhood education who have used the experimental edition of the ITL Program during the past ten years suggests that there is merit in a structured approach to early learning.

The insights of Dr. J. McVicker Hunt into the effects of circumstance and experience upon the formation of intellect in very young children and the Uzgiris-Hunt Ordinal Scales of Infant Psychological Development inspired by the research of Swiss psychologist Jean Piaget form the theoretical basis for the sequence of learning activities I have presented in this program.[5] I have been influenced by Hunt's concern with the "problem of the match" as it relates to the child's previous experience and by his discussion of the importance of early learning as it refers to the development of schemas and of intrinsic motivation in very young children. Along these lines I have attempted to match appropriate toys and educational materials to specific developmental levels in order to ensure successful early learning and to foster what can almost be termed a learning ego—the self-image of a child who *knows* he can learn.

The suggested toys and materials included in this book, *INFANT/TODDLER: Introducing Your Child to the Joy of Learning*, stress experience in sensorimotor development, particularly eye/hand coordination. Children learn by doing, by doing often, and by doing often in a setting which provides pleasurable reinforcement. As the young child acts upon these materials, intellectual development begins to take form. He associates identifying and defining words supplied by his or her parent/teacher with the actions he or she performs. Finally the child connects these experiences into a repertoire of behavior which we measure as intelligence. The research which led to the publication of this program indicates that when a very young child is taken through the continuum of experiences represented here, his or her intellectual development as measured by standardized tests is accelerated. My experience also indicates that the earlier you initiate this program, the better are the results. Beginning then with *mouthing*, the infant moves through twenty levels which include such developmental landmarks as *visual following, releasing or letting go, fitting parts to form a whole,* and *matching,* and completes the program with schemas that typically appear at the approximate age of three years. These developmental levels are more clearly defined in the introduction which follows as is the teaching style required to ensure the young learner's success.

Earladeen D. Badger, Ph. D.
Cincinnati, Ohio
May 1981

---

[1] The scores of these children on standardized measures are compared to those of a matched group and to those of a sibling control group by M. B. Karnes, J. A. Teska, A. S. Hodgins and E. D. Badger in "Educational Intervention at Home by Mothers of Disadvantaged Infants," *Child Development* (December, 1970) 925-935.

[2] I have reported on this field-testing experience in two articles. The first, "A Mother's Training Program—the Road to a Purposeful Existence," appeared in *Children* (September-October, 1971) 168-173. The second, "A Mother's Training Program—A Sequel Article" appeared in the same journal, renamed *Children Today* (May-June, 1972) 7-11.

[3] The results of this research are presented in a monograph entitled, "Psychological Development of Orphanage-Reared Infants: Interventions With Outcomes" by J. McV. Hunt, K. Mohandessi, and M. Akiyanna and appear in Genetic Psychology Monographs, 94:177, 1976.

[4] I have reported on the positive effects of the Program on 12-month infants of teenage mothers in a chapter entitled "The Infant Stimulation/Mother Training Project" in *Infant Education* (Eds.) B. Caldwell and D. Stedman. New York: Walker Publishing Co., 1977, 45-62.

[5] Dr. Hunt is best known for his scholarly book, *Intelligence and Experience* (New York: Ronald Press, 1961) which has had a strong influence on government policy and programs in early childhood education. The Uzgiris-Hunt Ordinal Scales of Infant Psychological Development are available in a text entitled *Assessment in Infancy: Ordinal Scales of Psychological Development.* Urbana: University of Illinois Press, 1976.

Contents

Introduction

My experience with very young children began with my own three children. As I recall, I was a typical, somewhat anxious mother—eager to speed up the development of my children by buying as many quality toys as I could afford. These were colorful, durable and fun to play with, but I often failed to select toys which matched the interest and ability levels of my youngsters. As my family grew up, I returned to graduate education, concentrating my studies on the learning styles and capabilities of very young children. My professional experience included a variety of educational programs for mothers and young children.

I spent five years creating and testing a developmental learning program for infants and toddlers which could be used successfully by mothers at home as well as teachers in child care programs. The result of my research was the *Infant/Toddler Learning Program.* The experimental edition of the *Infant/Toddler Learning Program,* which was targeted for use in early learning centers, was packaged in kit form. There was an infant kit (birth to 18 months) and a toddler kit (18-36 months). Each kit contained its own Teacher's Guide and all of the toys and materials needed to implement the program. That was ten years ago, however, when there was a paucity of early learning materials available for over-the-counter purchase. Since then, parenting programs have grown like topsy and toy manufacturers have responded by marketing basic toys which are durable, safe, and of high quality. That parents today are eager to know what toys to buy and how to proceed in fostering the intellectual development of their newborn child was recently dramatized for me. An article entitled "Head Start Beginning in the Nursery" *(Psychology Today,* September 1979), resulted in hundreds of letters and phone calls from prospective and new parents who wanted to order the *Infant/ Toddler Learning Program.* This book, *INFANT/ TODDLER: Introducing Your Child to the Joy of Learning,* occurred largely in response to their suggestions after reviewing the experimental edition of the *Infant/Toddler Learning Program.*

INFANT/TODDLER: Introducing Your Child to the Joy of Learning suggests appropriate toys and instructional materials with a detailed "how-to-do-it" teaching format. It is a program organized into twenty units representing a child's developmental levels from shortly after birth through three years of age. The toys and other learning materials mentioned in this book are identified by brand name and manufacturer as a guide to your purchase of appropriate toys.

INFANT/TODDLER sequences the activities for you and provides you with a step-by-step presentation for each of the program materials, as well as suggestions for enriching each experience through imaginative use of items found in the home. Progress indicators at the end of each activity help you evaluate your child's mastery of one developmental level before moving him or her on to the next. This *matching of learning experiences to the child's abilities* is one of the keys to ensuring successful learning with very young children. Parents as well as child-care workers sometimes expect too little from the child; more often they expect too much from him or her. When expectations are too low, the child loses interest rapidly; but when they are unrealistically high, the infant or toddler gives up and may even establish a sense of failure that grows with each unsuccessful effort. On the other hand, motivation to succeed and to achieve can be encouraged—even conditioned—when you provide learning experiences at a very early age which are matched to the youngster's abilities.

As you proceed through this program, you will learn many ways to help and encourage your child. For example, you will learn how to break down complex learning operations into small parts and to present each part to your child before expecting him or her to complete the entire task independently. By reducing your child's chance of mistakes and emphasizing his or her successes during these early years, you will produce the self-motivation which will help your child succeed in later learning experiences.

The *active involvement of the parent-teacher* is another key to the success of the program. While most parents and teachers of very young children recognize the importance of early learning experiences, they often fail to understand the importance of their relationship with the learner. Some say "Provide interesting toys and leave the child alone." But what about the imitative learning of the infant who claps his or her hands in response to the block tower his or her mother or father has built, or the toddler who pushes a car along the floor, imitating a motor sound, after he or she has observed an older brother or sister at play? What about the effects of a mother's praise and encouragement as her toddler strings beads or assembles a simple puzzle?

True, all children probably will learn these skills eventually, but those who develop to their fullest potential usually do so because recognition, encouragement and help are readily available.

The *Infant/Toddler Learning Program* has proven itself to be effective and fun for the parent-teacher and for the children in my applied research projects, and I believe you will find it equally rewarding as you work and learn with your own child.

Using *INFANT/TODDLER: Introducing Your Child to the Joy Of Learning*

Your child's success is assured by the organization the learning experiences into a sequence in which the mple activities of the early levels provide the founda- on for the later, more complex skills, by matching the tivities with the ability level of your child, and most nportant, by actively involving you in the learning rocess.

The quality of your relationship with your child is critical to his or her development. If you are warm and affectionate and follow these simple teaching practices, you will be an effective teacher.

1. *Be positive in your approach.* Acknowledge your child's success in each new task, even when he or she simply tries to do what you have demonstrated or asked. Minimize his or her mistakes and show him or her the right way immediately. Encourage your child to attempt the task again and praise his or her efforts.

2. *Break more complicated operations into separate steps.* Present one step at a time, beginning with the simplest. Do not go on to the next step until the child has been successful with the preceding one.

3. *Develop a good working relationship with your child based on mutual respect.* If your child does not pay attention or try to do as you have asked (and you are quite certain he or she can do what you have asked), put the toys away until later. Do not scold, beg or bribe. This time together should be fun for both of you. Many activities in the learning program encourage your toddler in free play, discovery and creativity. Be as enthusiastic about his or her free productions as you were when he or she followed your demonstration and instructions.

You will find that the format used to present each activity is simple to follow and helps you to organize he time you spend with your child. Each activity begins with a brief statement of the **Learning Operation—** the *primary* outcome of the new learning experience. Of course, there will be other learning as well. *Repetition of previous learning,* for example, is important in helping the young child truly master an operation or fully understand an idea. Perhaps equally important, youngsters build self-confidence through repetition at the mastery level. *Incidental learning* is also inherent in many activities, as when your toddler notes the sound a toy makes as it drops to the floor or perceives with his or her fingers the size and shape differences among wooden beads long before you have introduced appropriate words to describe these differences. *Discovery learning* cannot always be predicted, but if you are a keen observer of your toddler's actions, you can capitalize on this kind of learning and extend an activity beyond its original intent.

The **Materials** list will enable you to have at hand exactly what is needed to carry out a given activity. If you prepare in advance, you will not find it necessary to interrupt yourself or your child during the presentation in order to get additional supplies.

The **Presentation** is carefully outlined so that you will feel organized and confident as you provide new learning experiences for your child. Advance preparation is noted when it is needed—usually it is not.

Time is often allowed for the youngster to **Preview** more complicated or interesting toys on his or her own terms so that he or she is ready to manipulate them in more structured ways later on. Some activities require a **Demonstration** or modeling action on the part of the parent-teacher; others allow for **Guided Discovery** by the child. In general, however, activities provide for both guided and independent practice of the learning operation. In the activities for children over twenty months, there is particular emphasis on language development and reinforcement. You will note, however, that this book also includes suggested language interactions under **Parallel Language Development.** This matching of language experiences to the child's developmental abilities is highlighted in the introduction to each of the twenty units.

Observing Progress will help you become an accurate and reliable observer of your child's performance. By answering the questions and following the appropriate suggestions, you will be moving with your child toward the test of mastery. If, as suggested, you take the time to note actions or responses which characterize your child's performance, you will have a unique and fascinating record of his or her progress as a young learner. These observations will help you to recognize your child's individuality. As this material accumulates, you will discover that you are able to characterize the learning style of your youngster quite accurately. You will also be able to point out important landmarks as, for example, when your child first demonstrated that he or she could correctly follow verbal requests without a visual cue or model given through your demonstration of the materials.

If you take the time to fill in the progress section of each activity, you will have a precise record of your child's performance, and you will also value the record as a very personal document which attests to the very special relationship you shared with your child during these early months of his or her life. Filling in the Developmental Profile Chart (Appendix I) will give you an unique profile of your child's development—the ages when he or she accomplished the skills and the amount of interest shown.

Variations require advance preparation on your part and minimum expense. Whenever possible, carry out the variations with your child. He or she needs additional opportunities to practice new skills and, even more importantly, to transfer them to other materials and different settings. Many of the variations can be adapted to ordinary household routines and require no scheduled effort on your part. These are, however, a highly significant kind of activity; for through them

your child demonstrates to you his or her learning flexibility and retention and, through them, you share in the spontaneous and creative learning that emerges from early organized experiences.

Supplementary Materials and Activities is most obviously addressed to teachers of young children. Teachers' annotations here will help them to incorporate other educational toys and materials, many of which are listed in the Appendix. In subsequent years, this record will help them to plan more complete experimental units focusing on given developmental levels. Parents may, however, enjoy using this space as a kind of diary of shared experiences dealing with a particular activity.

The final section, **Recommended Toys,** lists toys which encourage practice and mastery of skills at each developmental level. When appropriate, toys are identified by brand name and manufacturer. When possible, several toys are suggested as options. If you are unable to locate a particular toy in your locale, you can refer to Appendix II where the addresses of toy manufacturers are provided.

Foreword

Many young women from every socio-economic background face the responsibility for their first-born young without any experience or tutelage in the care of young infants. Ideally, the spontaneous actions of infants should serve as the guide for mothers or caregivers to respond in a fashion that pleases the infant and fosters his or her development. Since many if not most mothers of first-born find their new responsibilities a wilderness of uncertainties, the structure provided by Dr. Badger's INFANT/TODDLER: Introducing Your Child to the Joy of Learning is a godsend that not only reduces the anxious uncertainties but fosters early

development and leads to a mutually joyous relationship that lays a fine foundation for future development.

Inasmuch as Dr. Badger has based her Infant and Toddler Learning Program on my own research and theorizing, I am very glad to find it published for wider distribution. It is very satisfying to have one's investigations and theoretical ideas put to practical use in fostering the development of infants and helping inexperienced young women cope with the anxious uncertainties of new motherhood.

Urbana, Illinois
J. McVicker Hunt, Ph.D.

MOUTHING

Your infant sees something to hold as something to put in his mouth. You will find that the mouthing objects offered here are just the right size for early hand-mouth experiences. These items are not to be compared with a nipple-like sucking pacifier, nor are they intended to quiet your baby. Rather, they provide varied mouthing experiences so he need not rely on his thumb or a pacifier.

Parallel Language Development. The love a mother has for her newborn infant is expressed in the way she meets his demands for attention. She learns quickly to discriminate between his cries of hunger, pain, or discomfort and how to respond to his vocalizations. The sound of your voice can soothe your newborn baby. He will become alert and begin to study your face if you talk to him in a rhythmical fashion. He is learning to focus his eyes and to become acquainted with you as he looks and listens.

ACTIVITY 1: Mouthing

Learning
Operation: The infant experiences the pleasure of mouthing.

Materials: Small rattle or teether

Presentation: *Guided Discovery.* When your infant is actively awake in his crib or infant seat, place the rattle in his hand. Do not be concerned whether it is the right or left hand. At first, he may hold it for only a few seconds and then drop it. Replace the rattle in his hand several times.

9

Independent Practice. On following days, continue to place the rattle in the infant's hand. Soon
he will bring the rattle to his mouth. At this stage
of development, something to hold becomes
something to put into the mouth. Introduce
the teether to add variety to the mouthing
experience.

OBSERVING PROGRESS

Does the infant drop the rattle the first
time it is placed in his hand?

☐ yes   ☐ no

If yes, continue to place it in his hand on
following days at times when he is
actively awake.

Does he rather consistently bring the
rattle directly to his mouth?

☐ yes   ☐ no

If yes, continue to provide experiences
with the rattle and the teether. Remember,
mouthing is a pleasurable activity to the
infant, and he will want to repeat this experience many times.

ACTIONS OR RESPONSES
I WOULD LIKE TO REMEMBER

_____

_____

_____

_____

TEST OF MASTERY: Given a teether,
the infant grasps it in his hand and easily,

without hesitation, brings it to his mouth
and sucks on it.

Infant's Age in Months at Mastery _____

VARIATION: Offer your baby a variety of objects to mouth—an old-fashioned,
wooden clothespin (not a clip-on pin), a
new plastic hair roller, a damp washcloth
or sponge. In choosing objects for mouthing, make certain that these objects are
easy to grasp, do not have sharp edges
and are nontoxic.

SUPPLEMENTARY MATERIALS
OR ACTIVITIES OF MY OWN

_____

_____

_____

_____

_____

RECOMMENDED TOYS

Variety of inexpensive baby rattles and
teethers (Baby World, Larco, Plakie, Sanitoy
and Stahlwood), *Happy Rattles** and *Happy
Teethers* (Playskool), *Teething Jack* (Child
Guidance)

*Happy Rattles is a registered trademark of Playskool, Inc.

VISUAL ATTENTION

Your infant sees and follows interesting objects with his eyes. The presentations here will introduce you to the importance of placing or holding interesting objects so that your baby can see them clearly, changing these objects to provide new visual experiences and moving them to encourage visual following. As you experiment with these materials, you will learn more about your baby. What especially interests him? How long does he remain interested? How long should you wait between presentations? Watch his hands move as he becomes excited by the sound of the rattle or the movement of the balloon. This non-directed use of his hands will develop into reaching and grasping.

Parallel Language Development. Your attachment to your infant is demonstrated in the way you hold, soothe, look at and talk to your infant. Your interactions with the infant, in turn, strengthen your attachment. Everyday caretaking activities, such as feeding, diapering, and bathing, provide an excellent opportunity for interaction to occur. When you are near the infant and make eye-to-eye contact, encourage the following interactions:

- As soon as your baby begins to make vowel sounds like *ah, ee,* or *oo* for extended periods, repeat his vocalizing patterns. Not only will he become more sociable as he plays this vocal game with you, but he will be encouraged to experiment in making new sounds.

- Feeding, diapering, and bathing your baby can be mechanical chores or they can be occasions to establish emotional closeness. If you are relaxed and chatter or sing to baby as you touch and massage his body, your baby will coo gleefully in response to your voice and touch. "This Little Piggie Goes to Market" and "Hickory, Dickory Dock" bring about delight and vocalization as you touch your baby.

ACTIVITY 1: Focusing

Learning Operation:

The infant focuses his eyes on interesting objects (for development of visual fixation).

Materials:

Cotton cord, colored plastic clothespins, smallest-size balloons, plastic pinwheel

Presentation:

Preparation. Attach the cotton cord from side to side across the crib in clothesline fashion so that objects tied to it will be approximately one foot from your infant's face. Alternately use a balloon and plastic pinwheel, securing each in place with a colored clothespin. (Remove the long handle from the plastic pinwheel and round the sharp edges with scissors before attaching to the cord.)

Guided Discovery. These objects are stimulating for the young infant to look at and are light enough to move gently within his view. If you blow lightly on them, their movement will increase the infant's attention and interest. A ten-minute presentation is long enough. Remove the mobile and repeat this procedure at different times on following days.

12

OBSERVING PROGRESS

Does the infant begin to focus his eyes on the balloon or plastic pinwheel for several seconds at a time?

☐ yes ☐ no

If not, attract his attention by blowing on the objects or shaking the cord to make them move gently.

☐ yes ☐ no

Does he seem to get excited, that is, increase the movement of his arms or legs or gurgle sounds when you repeat the presentation?

☐ yes ☐ no

If yes, reinforce his pleasure in recognizing the mobile by repeating his sounds, smiling and talking to him. You may wish to incorporate new materials as suggested in the VARIATION.

ACTIONS OR RESPONSES I WOULD LIKE TO REMEMBER

_____

_____

_____

TEST OF MASTERY: Given interesting objects attached to a mobile, the infant focuses his eyes on them for several seconds at a time and demonstrates his pleasure by gurgling and moving his arms and legs.

Infant's Age in Months at Mastery ———

VARIATIONS: As the infant begins to experience pleasure in "looking" at the balloons and the plastic pinwheels, introduce colorful swatches of fabric cut in circular or square shapes approximately six inches across. A chiffon scarf, plastic streamers, or colorful pictures are other examples of materials that your infant will look at with interest.

You may choose to attach a wooden dowel, one inch in diameter, across the crib. If you have an electric drill, holes can be made to attach the rod to one side of the crib from which you can hang interesting visual material. Use heavy cotton yarn to suspend the materials.

RECOMMENDED TOYS

Busy Bee Mobile (Stahlwood)

Butterfly Mobile (Stahlwood)

Butterfly & Bee Mobile (Child Guidance)

ACTIVITY 2: Visual Following

Learning Operation: The infant develops controlled eye movement when following moving objects.

Materials: Large rattle
Squeaker toy

Presentation: *Focusing Attention.* With your infant in an infant seat or lying in his crib, attract his attention by shaking the rattle approximately one foot from his face.

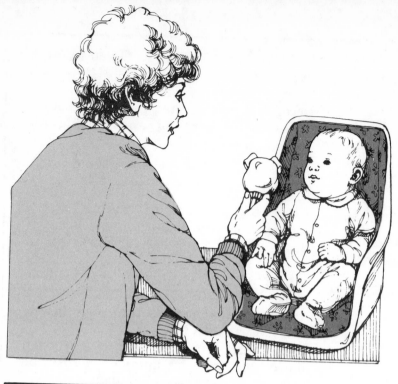

Guided Practice. When he fixes his eyes on the rattle, slowly move it in a 180° arc (a half circle). Use the same technique to show the infant a squeaker toy. By changing the object, you will hold the infant's interest longer. And if he prefers looking at you and studying your lips as you speak, do not be surprised. Mother's face and voice are more interesting than a squeaky toy during an infant's first months of life.

OBSERVING PROGRESS

Does the infant quickly focus his eyes on the rattle when you shake it?

☐ yes   ☐ no

If not, continue using the activity with the changing mobile on page 12 until the infant watches the objects for several seconds. Remember, your infant must be able to fix his attention on an object for several seconds before he can learn to follow a moving object.

If yes, does he follow the rattle with his eyes and his head as you move it in an arc?

ACTIONS OR RESPONSES
I WOULD LIKE TO REMEMBER

_____

_____

_____

_____

_____

TEST OF MASTERY: Given a moving object about one foot from the infant's face, he fixes his eyes on it and follows its movement accurately with his eyes.

Infant's Age in Months at Mastery _____

VARIATION: A set of keys, a beaded necklace, and beans or buttons in a closed container are other objects which your baby will enjoy following with his eyes. The interesting sounds of these objects help to attract and hold his attention.

SUPPLEMENTARY MATERIALS
OR ACTIVITIES OF MY OWN

_____

_____

_____

_____

RECOMMENDED TOYS

Variety of inexpensive larger rattles and squeeze toys (Baby World, Larco, Plakie, and Stahlwood)

Play Pets (Playskool)

Squeaker Creatures (Child Guidance)

Baby's Doll (Playskool)

EARLY EYE/HAND COORDINATION

Your infant sees something to hold as something to bang or shake. As he begins to coordinate the use of eyes and hands and to reach and grasp, he is ready for the crib exercisor (gym) and for small objects to shake and bang. He will enjoy the sounds he is able to produce, and the use of these toys marks the beginning of his control in the manipulation of objects.

Parallel Language Development. You move naturally from baby talk and vocal games with your infant to more informative sentences. "Now, I'm washing your ears", and you emphasize ears as the washcloth touches the ear in the course of caretaking activities. You also experiment in introducing new consonant sounds, such as *ah-goo, boo,* for your baby to imitate. In spite of the limited feedback on the part of the infant at this stage of his development, you are encouraged to continue to introduce new sounds and to emphasize key words even though your infant is unable to repeat the new sounds or words. You must realize that your baby absorbs and understands much more than he is able to express. This marks the beginning of receptive language.

ACTIVITY 1: Purposeful Grasping

Learning
Operation: The infant grasps intentionally in response to an action-reward toy.

Materials: Crib exercisor (gym)

Presentation: *Preparation.* Provide playtime with the crib exercisor when your infant is actively awake and at those times when you are not free to play with him. Attach the crib exercisor to the sides of the crib two or three times a day for periods of ten to twenty minutes rather than for one long period of time each day.

15

Independent Discovery and Practice. In the beginning, your infant may accidentally hit the exercisor as he moves his arms or legs causing it to produce an interesting sound. He will soon learn, however, to grasp the units intentionally in order to hear the accompanying sounds and to experience the satisfaction of muscle tension and release.

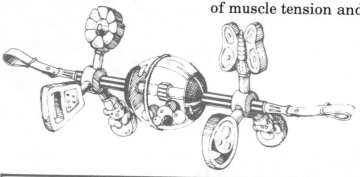

OBSERVING PROGRESS

Does the infant at first accidentally hit one of the grasping units as he moves his arms or legs?

☐ yes   ☐ no

If yes, does he seem to get excited? Does he increase the movement of his arms and legs when he hears the accompanying sounds of shaking beads and bells?

After several sessions with the crib exercisor, does he purposefully grasp one of the units and shake it?

☐ yes   ☐ no

If not, repeat the mouthing activities which also provide practice in grasping an object.

If yes, continue to provide other opportunities for play with other noise-making objects as suggested in the VARIATION.

ACTIONS OR RESPONSES I WOULD LIKE TO REMEMBER

_____

_____

_____

TEST OF MASTERY: Given an action-reward toy, the infant purposefully grasps the toy to make it produce a sound.

Infant's Age in Months at Mastery _____

VARIATION: A number of crib exercisors are commercially available. Most make accompanying sounds which are in themselves pleasurable and reinforce the infant's interest in grasping or even kicking at the movable parts. Their limitation, of course, is that their use is restricted to the crib, and you might find your infant becoming bored with only one. You can vary the activity by using a cotton cord or wooden dowel across the crib and tying sound-producing objects, such as rattles, bells, aluminum pie plates, or measuring spoons, to it.

SUPPLEMENTARY MATERIALS OR ACTIVITIES OF MY OWN

_____

_____

RECOMMENDED TOYS

Variety of inexpensive crib exercisors (Baby World, Sanitoy and Stahlwood)

Deluxe Baby Gym (Sanitoy)
Jumping Jack Scarecrow (Fisher-Price)
Play Gym (Fisher-Price)

Semper Baby toys (also known as *Fischerform)* which are available at certain toy stores include a sturdy line of crib and floor mounts with a number of interesting apparatuses that your infant can look at and activate. These are expensive, imported from Sweden, and I recommend them for use in infant daycare centers and for parents looking for high quality, educational total unit concept for their infant.

ACTIVITY 2: Banging and Shaking

Learning Operation: Banging and shaking small objects with vertical and horizontal motions.

Materials: Two wooden blocks
Large rattle

Presentation: *Demonstration and Guided Practice.* Seat your infant in his high chair or infant table. Attract his attention by using a vertical motion to bang a block on the table surface and encourage him to pick it up and bang it. Express your delight if he imitates your banging motion and encourage him to repeat the banging operation. He may enjoy having you join him in this banging activity, so feel free to use the second block to accompany him.

Demonstrate the use of the rattle, shaking it in a horizontal motion. The sound will attract your infant's attention. Give the rattle to him and encourage him to shake it.

Pick up the two blocks and bang them together. Repeat with enthusiasm. Place the blocks on the table surface and encourage your infant to pick them up and imitate your actions. Do not be surprised or discouraged if it is necessary to repeat this demonstration several times on following days. These motions are more precise and difficult than those required merely to bang a block on the table.

Independent Practice. The infant has begun to understand that something to hold can also become something to bang or shake. He will soon expand his banging and shaking skills and will use them with new as well as with familiar toys and materials. Other suggestions are given in the VARIATION (see page 18).

OBSERVING PROGRESS

Does the infant alternate between banging and mouthing these objects?

☐ yes   ☐ no

If yes, you can be sure that he is torn between the pleasure of mouthing and banging. Do not be concerned. Continue to demonstrate the banging and shaking actions.

Does he make a motion similar to a vertical (up and down) motion as he bangs or hits the block on the table surface?

☐ yes   ☐ no

If yes, recognize his efforts by smiling and clapping your hands or by praising him.

If not, continue to demonstrate the action on following days. Be deliberate, almost slow, in your movements, but maintain enthusiasm.

Does the infant make a horizontal (back and forth) motion as he shakes the rattle?

☐ yes   ☐ no

If yes, praise him.

If not, continue to demonstrate. It may help to put your hand over his as he holds the rattle and guide him through the horizontal shaking motion.

Does the infant bang the two blocks together?

☐ yes   ☐ no

If not, provide him with two blocks and watch how he manipulates them. Does your observation give you any ideas of how to help the infant? The infant may, for example, have difficulty in picking up two blocks, one in each hand. Help him by handing him the blocks one at a time. If he can hold the blocks securely, put your hands over his and help him to strike the two blocks together. Playing "Pat-a-Cake" or other hand-clapping games with your baby will also help him to develop the precision needed to hit the two blocks together.

ACTIONS OR RESPONSES I WOULD LIKE TO REMEMBER

_____

_____

_____

TEST OF MASTERY: Given a small wooden block, the infant grasps it firmly and, using a vertical motion, pounds the block on the table surface. Given two blocks, he is able to pick them up, one in each hand, and strike them together. Given a rattle, he uses a horizontal motion to produce sounds.

Infant's Age in Months at Mastery _____

VARIATION: Encourage your infant to practice these new skills with other objects. A metal or wooden spoon makes a good pounding toy for use while seated in his high chair or in combination with a metal cooking pot for pounding play on the floor. He will enjoy shaking a small, sealed plastic container into which you have placed dried beans, marbles or pebbles. Small bells on a handle, tied to a shoelace, or firmly stitched to a strip of cloth are also satisfying shaking toys.

SUPPLEMENTARY MATERIALS OR ACTIVITIES OF MY OWN

_____

_____

_____

RECOMMENDED TOYS

Cubical counting blocks—six colors in a box—are recommended for small hands (Milton-Bradley or Ideal). Can be purchased at educational supply stores or from toy catalogs.

Disney Wood Blocks (Playskool)

Wood ABC Blocks (Stahlwood)

Gus the Walrus for horizontal shaking (Fisher-Price), _Baby Rattle_ #535 (Sanitoy) and _Ring Rattle_ (Fischerform)

EARLY COGNITION: INTEREST IN OBJECTS

Toys designed to respond to the infant's actions develop the child's ability to control his environment. The child's play with these toys demonstrates how intentional actions are beginning to replace random activity. You will notice his curiosity and sustained interest as he becomes involved with these materials. During the hide-and-seek game, you will see what Dr. J. McVicker Hunt calls "the emergence of Object Construction"—now, something out of sight is not out of mind.

Parallel Language Development. As your infant's awareness and understanding of his world increases, you will need to expand your verbal interactions. Begin to recite nursery rhymes, do finger games, and play "pat-a-cake" and "peek-a-boo" on a daily basis. These activities are important to his understanding of language for they provide opportunities for the baby to hear differences in sounds, word patterns and intonations. You will readily capture his interest and attention due to the rhythm and timing offered in these activities. And his emotional bodily responses will soon be followed by his attempts at repeating the sounds.

ACTIVITY 1: Action-Responses

Learning Operation:

Securing a response from a toy through a repeated hitting action.

Materials:

Suction toy
Musical ball (Stahlwood or Fisher-Price)

Presentation:

Demonstration and Guided Practice. Seat your infant in his high chair or on your lap, facing the table. Secure the suction toy on the table surface. Hit the toy to set it in motion. As the infant delights in hearing the rattling sound produced and watching the toy's movement, continue to hit the toy to maintain the sound and movement. Share your child's interest and excitement. After you've demonstrated the hitting action several times, encourage him to hit the toy.

Put your infant in a crawling position on the floor. Sit down beside him and place the musical ball in front of him within his arm's reach. Demonstrate how hitting the ball will cause it to roll and produce sounds. Encourage the infant to hit at the ball in order to set it in motion.

Independent Practice. Your baby will enjoy opportunities to play with the suction toy before and after feeding times while he is seated in his highchair. The musical ball will be a favorite for floor play.

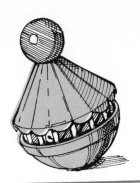

OBSERVING PROGRESS

Does the infant intentionally hit the suction toy to make it move and continue to hit it to keep it in motion?

☐ yes   ☐ no

If not, repeat your demonstration when you are certain he is watching you. Accentuate the hitting motion by raising your hand to shoulder level before following through.

Does the infant hit at the musical ball in order to set it in motion?

☐ yes   ☐ no

If not, make certain that the ball is close enough to his hand so that he can accidentally hit it and produce movement and sounds.

ACTIONS OR RESPONSES I WOULD LIKE TO REMEMBER

_____

_____

_____

TEST OF MASTERY: Given an action-response toy, the infant is able to repeat the hitting action necessary to set and keep the toy in motion for several minutes.

Infant's Age in Months at Mastery _____

VARIATION: A roly-poly toy or a plastic ball with movable objects inside will produce similar interest and activity from your baby. A musical top or crank music box are also interesting action-response toys, but pushing the toy lever down and turning the crank are more difficult motor skills and better belong at DEVELOPMENTAL LEVEL 6 (see page 30). You can construct a suitable home-made action-response toy by carefully sealing a few marbles or dried beans inside an empty oatmeal box, a coffee can, or potato chip tube. While your baby is in a crawling position on the floor, he will enjoy hitting at the box, causing it to roll and setting the marbles or beans into motion.

SUPPLEMENTARY MATERIALS OR ACTIVITIES OF MY OWN

_____

_____

_____

RECOMMENDED TOYS

Variety of inexpensive suction toys (Baby World, Plakie, and Stahlwood)

Roly Poly toys (Baby World and Plakie), *Preinflated toys* (Stahlwood), *Roll Back toy* (Stahlwood), and *Softee Jingle Ball* (Stahlwood) all respond to a simple hitting motion.

Stay Put* Suction Cup Rattles (Playskool)

Big Bird Chime Mirror (Child Guidance)

Flutter Ball (Playskool)

Big Bird Tumble Ball (Child Guidance)

Musical Ball (Stahlwood) (Fisher-Price)

Rota Rattle Suction Toy (Ambi)

Rock 'n' Roll Ball (Ambi)

*Stay Put is a trademark of Playskool, Inc.

ACTIVITY 2: Hide and Seek

Learning Operation:

The infant learns to find a hidden object, recognizing that it exists even when it is out of sight. This is known as objec[t] permanence and is an early sign of cognitive learning.

Materials:

A hiding cloth (large handkerchief or dish towel). Any box larg[e] enough to cover one of the following listed toys: small toy[s] used in earlier presentations, such as a rattle, squeaker, or a favorite small stuffed animal.

Presentation:

Focusing Attention.   Face your baby as the two of you sit on the floor or rug. Present him with one of the toys which is especially interesting and familiar to him. Let him look at and feel the toy.

Guided Discovery.   As he watches you, take the toy and partially hide it under the cloth within easy reach of your infant. Encourage him to get the toy. If he successfully finds it, repeat the game with excitement. After several finds, completely cover the toy with the cloth. Again, tell him to get or find the toy.

Guided Practice.   The child's joy of discovery will make him want to repeat the hidden object game again and again. Change the object occasionally using any small toy which interests him. Substitute a box for the cloth as the cover for the toy and encourage the child to look under the box. Further suggestions are given in the VARIATION.

OBSERVING PROGRESS

Does the infant find the toy when it is partially hidden?

☐ yes ☐ no

If not, repeat the presentation using other interesting toys. A favorite stuffed animal or doll may give him an extra reason to find the toy.

Does the infant locate the toy when it is completely hidden?

☐ yes ☐ no

If not, repeat the game being careful to only partially hide the object until he finds the object without hesitation.

Does he knock over the box or lift it in order to find the toy?

☐ yes ☐ no

If not, show him how you can lift the box and find the toy. Repeat the presentation.

ACTIONS OR RESPONSES I WOULD LIKE TO REMEMBER

_____

_____

_____

_____

_____

TEST OF MASTERY: Given the opportunity to observe a toy as it is hidden beneath a cloth or a box, the child is able to find the toy by removing the cover.

Infant's Age in Months at Mastery _____

VARIATION: Extend this series of hiding games by playing "peek-a-boo" (covering your face with your hands), rolling a ball out of the child's reach and view (behind a chair) and encouraging him to creep and find it, or placing a favorite finger food (a cracker or a section of an orange) behind his dish when he is seated in his high chair. Remember, you must have his attention and offer objects in which he is interested if you are to succeed with these hiding games.

SUPPLEMENTARY MATERIALS OR ACTIVITIES OF MY OWN

_____

_____

_____

_____

_____

RECOMMENDED TOYS

A favorite toy which is small enough to hide under a large handkerchief is all you need. Small stuffed dolls or animals (Baby World, Plakie, and Stahlwood) are especially good for partial hiding because they are more easily recognizable to a baby when the head is exposed.

SIMPLE MOTOR SKILLS

Your infant develops the coordinated motor skills of pushing and pulling and progresses to finer finger movements as he manipulates the parts of the busy box. Finally, he uses both hands to experience the properties of materials through stroking, crumpling, tearing, squeezing and pulling.

Parallel Language Development. Oddly enough, consonant sounds like *ba-ba* or *ah-goo* may first be heard as your infant is busily manipulating objects in his environment. Around the middle of the first year, babies seem to be most interested in making speech sounds when they are exploring objects. Begin to use a tape recorder to record these sounds and play them back to him. Do not miss this opportunity to also describe the characteristics of objects your child is manipulating or to name familiar persons, places, or things as he experiences them. He needs to become familiar with the language which matches and describes his actions.

ACTIVITY 1: Pushing and Pulling

Learning
Operation: Pushing and pulling an action toy.

Materials: Rattle ball (Fisher-Price)

Presentation: *Demonstration.* Place your baby in a crawling or sitting position on the floor or rug area. Sit beside or behind him and slowly pull the toy toward him and then slowly push it back. Share his pleasure in the sound and movement produced by this action.

Guided Practice. Now put the toy in front of him with the handle within his reach. Encourage him to grasp the handle of the toy with you so that he can begin to experience the pushing and pulling actions.

Independent Practice. When you feel that the child is helping you to pull and push, encourage him to move the toy by himself. Be enthusiastic about the action he makes.

OBSERVING PROGRESS

At first, does the infant try to shake or bang the push and pull toy?

☐ yes ☐ no

If yes, remember that he is only repeating actions he has already learned. Continue to demonstrate the pushing and pulling motions with the toy.

Does the infant release the handle before he has completed the forward pull and the push away actions?

☐ yes ☐ no

If yes, try to have his hand ride along with yours as you pull the toy forward and push it back. It may help to draw attention to the two motions if you slowly repeat the words *push-sh-sh* and *pull-ll-ll* at the same time you produce the action.

ACTIONS OR RESPONSES I WOULD LIKE TO REMEMBER

_____

_____

_____

_____

_____

TEST OF MASTERY: Given a push and pull toy, the child grasps the handle securely and purposefully pulls the toy toward himself and then pushes it away.

Infant's Age in Months at Mastery _____

VARIATION: Any long-handled push and pull toy will interest your baby and help him coordinate pushing and pulling motions. A pan with a handle also can be used. Let your infant play with the pan on the kitchen floor rather than on a rug surface so that he can make interesting sounds. Attach a string to a rattle and show him how to pull the string in order to get the rattle. There are also many commercially available string pull toys that he will be able to manipulate and enjoy at this stage of development.

SUPPLEMENTARY MATERIALS OR ACTIVITIES OF MY OWN

_____

_____

_____

_____

RECOMMENDED TOYS

Corn Popper (Fisher-Price)

String toys, such as *Toot Toot Engine, Queen Buzzy Bee* and *Bob-Along Bear* (Fisher-Price)

Slinky* Pull Toys (James Industries)

*Slinky is a registered trademark of James Industries, Inc.

ACTIVITY 2: Finger Motions

Learning Operation: Hitting, sliding, pushing and turning movable parts.

Materials: Busy Box (Child Guidance, Fisher Price)

Presentation:

Guided Discovery. Seat your baby on the floor in front of the busy box or place it in front of him when he is in a creeping position. You will need to hold and steady the box so that both of his hands are free to explore the toy. Demonstrate the hitting, sliding, pushing, and turning motions he will need to imitate to produce each of the sounds. Since a hitting motion is the easiest for the child to do, encourage him to imitate that action first.

Independent Discovery. As your baby meets with success and enjoys the actions he is able to produce, he will begin to manipulate the other movable parts of the busy box. Allow time for his independent exploration, and share your child's delight in discovering the motions needed to produce a response. If the infant is not successful in performing all the busy box activities after many opportunities to practice, introduce them in order of difficulty (hitting, sliding, pushing and turning), and praise his efforts in trying a difficult action by saying, for example, "Good. You're trying to turn the handle."

Independent Practice. Encourage your child to play freely with the busy box as you put it out from time to time. He will master all the actions called for if he has time to practice and as he learns to vary his finger movements.

OBSERVING PROGRESS

Does the infant seem primarily interested in performing the hitting and pushing activities?

☐ yes ☐ no

If yes, remember that these two activities are the easiest to set into motion.

Does the infant keep on trying to do the more difficult activities?

☐ yes ☐ no

If no, continue to show the child how to perform these activities on following days. Help your child by guiding his hand through each action. Share his enthusiasm as he masters each new activity.

If yes, continue to provide practice time when the child plays on his own.

ACTIONS OR RESPONSES I WOULD LIKE TO REMEMBER

_____

_____

_____

TEST OF MASTERY: Given the busy box, the child hits, slides, pushes, and turns the moveable parts.

Infant's Age in Months at Mastery _____

VARIATION: There are many commercial activity boxes which can be attached to the side of a crib. At this stage of development, however, a crib should be used for sleeping and not as a playpen.

As your infant is able to sit without support and to creep and crawl, you should child-proof your home so he is free to safely follow you from room to room. In so doing, he will find door stops to manipulate, knobs to pull, drawers to open, and doors to close. You will need to supervise him closely as he begins to explore his larger environment, but this freedom to learn by discovery should not be denied him.

SUPPLEMENTARY MATERIALS OR ACTIVITIES OF MY OWN

_____

_____

_____

_____

_____

RECOMMENDED TOYS

Peek 'n' See, Touch 'n' See, and *Hear 'n' See* (Child Guidance)

Disney Busy Poppin' Pals (Child Guidance)

*Clik-Clak Duck** or *Clik-Clak Puppy** (Playskool)

Frisky Frog (Fisher-Price)

Activity Center (Fisher-Price)

Turn and Learn Activity Center (Fisher-Price)

*See 'n' Say** (Mattel)

*Clik-Clak Duck and Clik-Clak Puppy are registered trademarks of Playskool, Inc.
*See 'n' Say is a registered trademark of Mattel, Inc.

ACTIVITY 3: New Perceptions

Learning Operation:

Using both hands to experience special characteristics of materials through stroking, crumpling, tearing, squeezing and pulling.

Materials:

Fur piece, tissue paper, foam rubber sponge, elastic strip, "feely box" (use a shoe box)

Presentation:

Preparation. Have your baby in a sitting position for these activities. Put the tactile materials in the "feely box" and set it aside so that he will not be tempted to explore all of these at one time.

Guided Demonstration and Imitation. Use the fur piece to show the infant a stroking motion. Pat the infant's cheek with the fur and rub it along his arm or leg. Murmur softly as you do this, *M-m-m-m-nice, So-so-o-oft* or similar words. Give him the fur piece and see what he does with it. Encourage him to feel it by petting, stroking or rubbing it against a part of his body. Repeat the murmuring words.

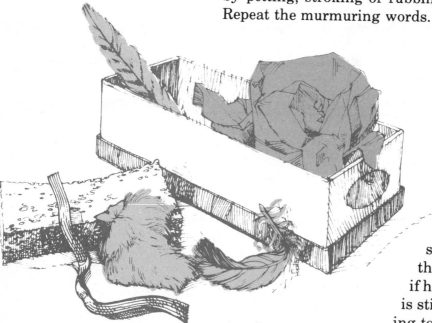

Use the piece of tissue paper to demonstrate crumpling. Then use both hands to pull on the tissue until it tears. Give the infant a piece of tissue and encourage him to crumple and tear it. Be enthusiastic about his efforts.

Use the foam rubber sponge to show a squeezing motion; use both hands. Give him the sponge and say, "You squeeze the sponge." Do not be concerned if he puts it in his mouth. Mouthing is still an important way of responding to unfamiliar materials.

Demonstrate the pulling action required to stretch the piece of elastic. Then give the infant one end of the elastic and gently pull on your end so that he feels the tug against his hand. Give him the elastic and see what he does with it.

Independent Exploration. Encourage your child to play freely with these materials from time to time. Occasionally, add new materials to his collection as suggested in the VARIATION. Above all, encourage the infant to feel common objects throughout the day.

Urge him to feel the sponge as you wipe off his feeding table; let him play with a sponge during his bath. Sponge or cloth balls or soft rubber animals are also fun to squeeze and chew. Allow him to finger the fur piece when he is drowsy or substitute a furry toy animal. Let him stroke a friendly kitten. Let him feel fur, angora, or feather trim on your clothing. Let him play with an ice cube.

OBSERVING PROGRESS

Does the infant use both hands to stroke and pat the fur piece, to crumple and tear the tissue paper, to squeeze the sponge, and to pull and stretch the elastic?

☐ yes ☐ no

If yes, your baby is making good progress in using both hands to explore and manipulate material and to learn new skills.

If not, continue to emphasize tactile exploration and provide additional experiences with the materials suggested in VARIATION.

ACTIONS OR RESPONSES I WOULD LIKE TO REMEMBER

_____

_____

_____

_____

TEST OF MASTERY: Given, in turn, a fur piece, a piece of tissue paper, a sponge, and a piece of elastic, the child uses both hands to experience the properties of these materials through stroking, crumpling, tearing, squeezing and pulling.

Infant's Age in Months at Mastery _____

VARIATION: Provide additional tactile experience by letting your baby handle coarse sandpaper, feathers, transparent tape, a plastic flower, tin foil, cotton balls, a scrap of velvet. Store them in the "feely box". Change and add items from time to time and provide access to new materials on a daily basis.

SUPPLEMENTARY MATERIALS OR ACTIVITIES ON MY OWN

_____

_____

_____

_____

RECOMMENDED TOYS

Inexpensive key rings (Baby World, Plakie, or Stahlwood)

Cracklee Animal (Stahlwood)

Infant comb and brush set (Plakie)

An *Animal Grabber* (Fisher-Price) can be included in your baby's "feely box" for added interest.

Infant Developmental Level

LETTING GO

After your infant has grasped, examined and manipulated the toys offered thus far in the presentations, he is ready to purposely drop objects and even to throw them. Beginning with the simple operation of releasing one object in order to pick up another, he prepares for the more forceful action of throwing. Finally, you will see how interested he becomes in dropping small objects into another large one such as a plastic bottle. With this early target toy, he combines purposeful grasping and releasing with fine eye/hand coordination.

Parallel Language Development.   Begin to connect the sounds your infant makes to familiar persons or objects—*Da-da* becomes daddy and *ba* is ball, while someone leaving the house is *bye-bye*. He begins to understand and respond to *no* if you use it selectively to protect him from danger. Encourage his early efforts in naming objects, family members, or pets by praising or hugging him if he tries to form words. Expect that only you will recognize his first attempts at naming things.

ACTIVITY 1: Releasing and Dropping

Learning Operation: Releasing one object in order to pick up another.

Materials: Three wooden blocks

Other small toys already familiar to the infant

Presentation: *Guided Discovery.* Seat your baby in his highchair or in front of you on the floor. Place two blocks on the floor in front of him. If he doesn't freely pick up a block in each hand, help him by handing the block to him. Hold each block close to the reach of each hand. Then take a third block and enthusiastically offer it to him. He must drop one block in order to take the third block.

Guided Practice. Provide him with additional experience in releasing objects by introducing as the third object a toy which is especially interesting to him—one he can't resist. Continue to play this game until your child can easily release one object in order to take another.

OBSERVING PROGRESS

Does the infant readily release one of the blocks in order to reach for and take the third block you're offering him?

☐ yes ☐ no

If yes, he is ready to play ball in the next activity.

If not, repeat this presentation at different times on following days until he willingly and easily releases one object to take another. Be certain that the third object you offer has appeal. If he has particular difficulty in letting go of objects, try offering a cracker or a cookie as the third item. When he purposefully begins to drop or throw things from his highchair, you are ready to help him transfer this action to the foam rubber ball in the next activity (see page 32).

**ACTIONS OR RESPONSES
I WOULD LIKE TO REMEMBER**

_____

_____

_____

TEST OF MASTERY: Given a block in each hand and offered an interesting third item, the child will release with ease one of the blocks in order to take the third object.

Infant's Age in Months at Mastery _____

VARIATION: After your baby has had many experiences in releasing one object in order to pick up another, you will notice that he begins to drop things from his highchair on purpose. It's such fun for him and a bother to a parent, but he is practicing a newly acquired skill. If you want to make this game easier on yourself, attach an interesting toy to a string which you have secured to the suction toy or to the side of the highchair. After your baby has dropped the toy overboard, he will learn to pull it up by the string. He can then play the dropping game by himself without needing you to keep picking up the toy.

**SUPPLEMENTARY MATERIALS
OR ACTIVITIES OF MY OWN**

_____

_____

_____

ACTIVITY 2: Throwing

Learning Operation: After learning to drop or release an object intentionally, the child masters the more forceful action of throwing.

Materials: Rubber ball, foam rubber ball or table tennis ball

Presentation: *Guided Practice.* Seat your baby on the floor and sit facing him approximately five feet away. Roll the ball to him and encourage him to return it to you. After several completed returns, throw the ball gently to him and again encourage him to return it to you.

Continue to play this game often on following days. Your child may want to roll the ball for many sessions before he attempts a throw. If he is walking, play the throwing game in a standing position. And, of course, you will want to play outdoors on pleasant days.

OBSERVING PROGRESS

Does the infant show interest in rolling or throwing the ball?

☐ yes   ☐ no

If not, continue to present the game in an enthusiastic manner. Be accepting if he hugs, nuzzles or mouths the ball. Perhaps you will want to provide additional practice in the release and dropping of objects as described in the previous activity (see page 31).

If he is attempting to throw the ball, does he merely drop it rather than use his whole arm for a real throw?

☐ yes   ☐ no

If yes, continue to practice. In time he will have the strength and coordination for a more forceful throw. You might try standing behind him and putting your hands over his as he holds the ball. Raise your arms together—up and out—pushing the ball from your hands as in a throwing motion.

If he is throwing the ball, does he seem to see the activity as a social game and enjoy playing it with you?

☐ yes   ☐ no

If not, be sure that you are responding with alertness and enthusiasm yourself. Maintain eye contact with him throughout the game. Encourage social interaction through praise and other related conversation: "Good throw! Now I'll throw the ball to you. Throw it back to me."

ACTIONS OR RESPONSES I WOULD LIKE TO REMEMBER

_____

_____

_____

_____

_____

TEST OF MASTERY: Given a foam rubber ball, the child will throw the ball to a responsive partner. In throwing the ball to someone, the child indicates that he recognizes the social aspects of the game.

Infant's Age in Months at Mastery _____

VARIATION: In your outings with your child, vary ball playing by providing a sponge ball. Whether you are in the yard or at a park, ball playing is a favorite game of every child. Long before he is able to walk, he will enjoy catching or retrieving the ball and carrying, rolling or throwing it back to you.

SUPPLEMENTARY MATERIALS OR ACTIVITIES OF MY OWN

_____

_____

_____

_____

ACTIVITY 3: Aiming and Finding a Target

Learning Operation:

The infant grasps, aims and drops clothespins into the mouth of a plastic bottle.

Materials:

A plastic milk bottle, old-fashioned wooden clothespins (not the wire-clip type)

Presentation:

Guided Practice.   Sit with your baby at a small table* or on the floor. Place the bottle in front of him and show him how to drop in a clothespin. Say, "In goes the clothespin. Now, YOU put one in the bottle."

If he imitates your action, praise him by saying, "Good! You did it."

If he fails to get the clothespin in, help him try again. Steady the bottle with your hand if he is knocking it over. You might try holding the opening of the bottle toward the clothespin if he is having considerable difficulty.

After he has successfully dropped several clothespins into the bottle, show him how to turn it upside down and shake it in order to get the clothespins out.

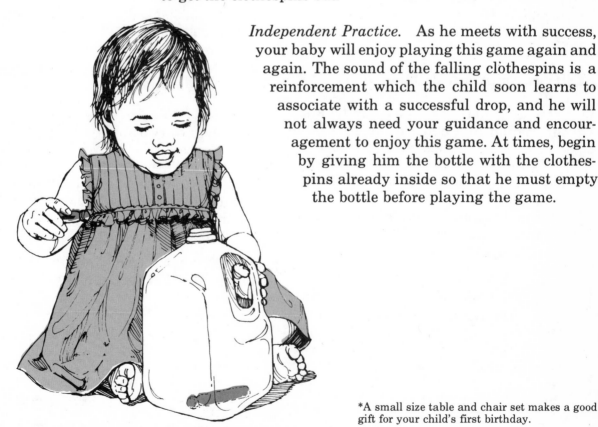

Independent Practice.   As he meets with success, your baby will enjoy playing this game again and again. The sound of the falling clothespins is a reinforcement which the child soon learns to associate with a successful drop, and he will not always need your guidance and encouragement to enjoy this game. At times, begin by giving him the bottle with the clothespins already inside so that he must empty the bottle before playing the game.

*A small size table and chair set makes a good gift for your child's first birthday.

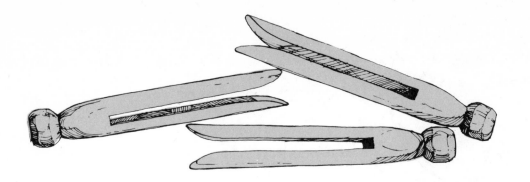

OBSERVING PROGRESS

Does the infant successfully drop the clothespins into the bottle most of the time?

☐ yes   ☐ no

If not, provide an easier version of the game by using a large-mouthed can as the container and reintroducing the plastic bottle later.

If yes, continue to play the game for fun and practice, then introduce the VARIATION.

ACTIONS OR RESPONSES I WOULD LIKE TO REMEMBER

_____

_____

_____

_____

TEST OF MASTERY: The child drops clothespins into a plastic bottle by carefully grasping, aiming and releasing each clothespin.

Infant's Age in Months at Mastery _____

VARIATION: Use an empty one- or two-pound coffee tin with a plastic lid to make this target toy. Cut a 1½″ circular hole in the center of the lid. Encourage your baby to drop clothespins, a rubber ball 1″ in diameter, or 1″ wooden blocks through this hole. Be sure to name the objects as he drops them into the can so that he continues to associate words with his actions. In order for him to remove the objects from the can, he must pull off the lid. He will enjoy trying to do this if you help by holding the can. You must fit the lid back on for him though, as this is too complex a task for him.

If your child easily fits objects through the hole in the lid of the empty tins, remove the lid and demonstrate how he can fit clothespins around the rim of the coffee tin. This is a more difficult task but challenging for the infant who is ready to tackle it.

SUPPLEMENTARY MATERIALS OR ACTIVITIES OF MY OWN

_____

_____

_____

_____

_____

RECOMMENDED TOYS

Fill 'n' Spill Bottle 'n' Hammer (Stahlwood or Baby World)

Crib and Playpen Puzzle Assortment (Fisher-Price)

Floating Family (Fisher-Price)

Milk Carrier (Fisher-Price)

7 Infant Developmental Level

SOCIALIZATION AND IMITATIVE BEHAVIOR

At this developmental level, your infant more clearly views himself and his actions in relation to others. His social nature is expressed as he looks at himself in a mirror and enjoys imitating your facial expressions. The infant uses the manipulative skills he mastered earlier along with developing social skills when playing with blocks and vehicles. Before your child can master early self-help skills, such as feeding and dressing himself, he must become aware of his own body and the relationship of its parts. As he becomes familiar with his body, he will use imitative behavior to acquire new skills for helping himself.

Parallel Language Development.   With encouragement, your infant will begin to imitate your actions and point to his eyes, nose, ears, and mouth if you provide the model and name and touch these parts on yourself. If you do this often, he will soon be able to touch the appropriate body part in response to your question, "Where is your nose?" While unable to say nose or eyes yet, he understands the meaning of the words, and he begins to respond to a verbal request.

CTIVITY 1: Mirroring Facial Expressions

Learning Operation: The infant experiences pleasure in looking at his mirror image and begins to imitate facial expressions.

Materials: Hand mirror

Presentation: *Guided Discovery and Imitation.* Place your baby in his highchair or hold him on your lap. Hold the mirror in front of his face and say, "Look, see the pretty baby."

Point to his face in the mirror. As he shows interest in looking at himself, make animated facial expressions and name the body part being used. Suggestions are listed below, but do not hesitate to add others of your own. Of course, you will not expect your child to master these at once.

- Smack your lips and say, "Kiss the baby."
- Open your mouth wide, point to it and say, "mouth".
- Blink your eyes, point to them and say, "eyes".
- Wrinkle your nose, point to it, and say, "nose".
- Pat your hair and say, "hair".
- Pull on one of your ears and say, "ear".

Guided Practice. Play the mirror game often. If a large mirror is available, your baby will enjoy being held up in front of it to play this social game with you. After diapering, feeding, or before bedtime, hold him in front of a large mirror in the bedroom or bathroom. As you hold him in your arms and your face is close to his, continue making facial expressions, and talk about related body parts. In the beginning, he will just look at the faces you make, but with repetition, he will begin to imitate them.

He will also enjoy sitting in front of a floor-length mirror as he plays with toys or merely observes himself.

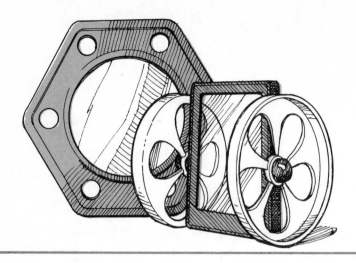

OBSERVING PROGRESS

Is the infant interested in looking at himself in a mirror?

☐ yes   ☐ no

If not, continue to hold him in front of a large mirror and to repeat the same facial expressions and name the related body parts on a daily basis.

If yes, encourage him to imitate your expressions. It may help, for example, if you touch his lips when you smack yours or point to his nose when you wrinkle yours. Show your delight if he babbles in response to your repeated commentary.

ACTIONS OR RESPONSES I WOULD LIKE TO REMEMBER

_____

_____

_____

_____

_____

TEST OF MASTERY: Given an opportunity to observe his image reflected in a mirror, the child responds with interest and visual alertness and is able to imitate facial expressions.

Infant's Age in Months at Mastery _____

VARIATION: Use your infant's doll or teddy bear to identify body parts. Point to the doll's eyes or the teddy bear's ears and say, "eyes" and "ears". Your infant will attend with interest if you alternate between the doll and yourself in touching and naming like body parts. Make the game rhythmical by touching and saying, "Here's the dolly's nose, and here's Mommy's (Daddy's) nose."

Don't forget to touch and name your child's nose, too.

SUPPLEMENTARY MATERIALS OR ACTIVITIES OF MY OWN

_____

_____

_____

_____

_____

RECOMMENDED TOYS

Mirror Rattle (Stahlwood or Baby World)

Look-at-Me-Elephant (Fisher-Price)

Flower Rattle (Fisher-Price)

Big Bird Chime Mirror (Child Guidance)

Busy Faces (Child Guidance)

ACTIVITY 2: Building a Tower

Learning Operation: Acquiring balancing and stacking skills in order to build a a tower of blocks.

Materials: Five wooden blocks

Presentation: *Demonstration and Discovery.* Sit with your infant on the floor or rug area and place the five blocks in front of you. Stack two or three blocks for him to see. Showing the infant how to knock down the tower will increase his interest in the activity.

Guided Practice. Continue to stack two or three blocks, saying, "Make a tower like mine."

As your child tries and succeeds, encourage him by saying, "Good! What a nice tower. Put another block on top."

When he knocks down his or your tower, clap your hands, act surprised, and say, "Boom! They all fell down!"

Continue to play this game often. As the infant becomes better at the game, his delight in both the building up and the knocking down will increase.

OBSERVING PROGRESS

Does the infant seem primarily interested in knocking down towers you build rather than in building his own?

☐ yes   ☐ no

If yes, be patient and continue to help him build his tower by handing him the blocks, one by one, and praising him as he tries. Don't be competitive; that is, don't always build a tower higher than he can build.

ACTIONS OR RESPONSES I WOULD LIKE TO REMEMBER

_____

_____

_____

_____

_____

TEST OF MASTERY: Given five blocks, the child demonstrates sufficient eye/hand coordination to build a three-block tower.

Infant's Age in Months at Mastery _____

VARIATION: Your baby can transfer these new skills to another situation if you give him three different sized cans to stack. The can tower will be taller than the block tower with the same amount of effort and will introduce the concept of size. Not insignificantly, the cans make a louder noise when knocked down, which adds to the fun. Of course, you will make certain that no sharp edges have been left on the open end of the cans. Perhaps you can collect a set of cans with reusable plastic lids so the cans may be stacked from either side and so there will be no danger of jagged edges.

SUPPLEMENTARY MATERIALS OR ACTIVITIES OF MY OWN

_____

_____

_____

RECOMMENDED TOYS

Same blocks recommended for Activity 2, Developmental Level 3 (page 17)

Stackable Shapes* (Tonka)

*Stackable Shapes is a trademark of Tonka Toys Division of Tonka Corporation.

ACTIVITY 3: Making Cars Go

Learning Operation: Controlling the movement and direction of wheeled toys by pushing.

Materials: Wooden car

Presentation: *Demonstration.* Sit with your baby on the floor or rug area. Get on your hands and knees to show him how you push the car around the room. Be sure to provide the *r-r-r-r* motor sound. Explain, "See how I make the car go! Now YOU make the car go."

Individual Practice. Give the child the wooden car. Let him examine it freely, but encourage him to push it on the floor. Providing the motor sound for him may be encouraging. If he makes a sound for the car, respond enthusiastically. If there's an older brother or sister participating in this kind of play, you can be certain that these imitative skills will develop faster.

Extension. After your child is successful in controlling the motion of the push car, give him the friction toy which moves by itself after an initial push. Demonstrate the slight push necessary to set the toy in motion. Infants do not immediately see the difference between the two kinds of movement, but with experience, they will learn how to use both and will enjoy playing with them.

OBSERVING PROGRESS
Does the infant succeed in pushing the car around the floor and does he enjoy doing so?

☐ yes ☐ no

If not, continue on other days to demonstrate and make the sounds.

If yes, does he say, "Car, car go", or, "r-r-r", when he plays with the car? If not, be sure to make the sound as he plays so that he learns to associate appropriate words with his actions.

ACTIONS OR RESPONSES
I WOULD LIKE TO REMEMBER

_____

_____

_____

_____

_____

TEST OF MASTERY: Given a wheeled toy, the child pushes it around on the floor, controlling its movement and direction and supplying a motor sound or other appropriate verbal responses. Given a friction toy, the child uses a small push to set it in motion.

Infant's Age in Months at Mastery _____

SUPPLEMENTARY MATERIALS
OR ACTIVTITIES OF MY OWN

_____

_____

_____

_____

RECOMMENDED TOYS
Click 'n' Clatter Car (Fisher-Price)
Henry Hippo (Fisher-Price)
Crawler Car (Fischerform)
Oscar (Brio)

ACTIVITY 4: Self-Help Skills

Learning Operation:
Performing simple actions on himself (brushing his hair, putting on and removing a necklace) in order to begin early self-help skills.

Materials:
Comb and brush
Snap-Lock Beads (Fisher-Price)

Presentation:
Preparation. Make a necklace by assembling the beads. Do this in advance and not in the presence of your child. Later, at DEVELOPMENTAL LEVELS 9 and 10, you will teach him how to push together and take apart these beads.

Demonstration. Put your baby in a sitting position. Take the brush and pretend to brush your hair. Say, "I can brush my hair."
Then slowly brush the child's hair and say, "I can brush your hair."

Guided Imitation. Hand the child the brush and say, "Can you brush your hair?"
He may want to brush your hair first. Be a sport and let him. Then encourage him again to brush his hair. Praise him as he tries, saying, "Good! You can brush your own hair."
Later, he may be interested in brushing his hair in front of a mirror. It is not important whether he correctly brushes his hair. In fact, your child may only manage to bring the brush to his head and make a sweeping motion.

Guided Practice. Put the necklace of beads over his head an encourage him to take it off. Initially he will be successf only in taking it off. After you play this game with him man times, he will try to put the necklace over his head by himsel As he tries, be sure to praise him, "What a smart baby! Yo can put the necklace on."

He will also enjoy looking at himself in a mirror whe playing with the necklace. The motions of putting on an taking off the circle of beads are similar to those whic he will use later in dressing and undressing himself.

OBSERVING PROGRESS

Does the infant imitate the self-help skills you demonstrate?

☐ yes ☐ no

If not, continue to show him the skills and also include those in the VARIATION and others of your own. Be enthusiastic and make the activities fun.

If yes, you are providing a good model and encouragement. As the child learns to complete an activity about himself, he is learning about the size and shape of his own body and how it fits into the space around him. This body awareness is necessary for him to learn the self-help skills of feeding, washing and dressing himself.

Does the child attempt on his own any of the self-help skills you have demonstrated?

☐ yes ☐ no

If not, be certain you are providing him with opportunities to try the skills on his own and praise for his efforts.

ACTIONS OR RESPONSES I WOULD LIKE TO REMEMBER

_____

_____

TEST OF MASTERY: The child brings the brush to his head and imitates a brushing motion and is able to put on and to remove the circle of beads.

Infant's Age in Months at Mastery _____

VARIATION: Extend the range of your child's self-help skills by giving him a washcloth and letting him take a few wipes at his face and hands before you do the real clean-up job. Be sure to provide words to describe his actions: "Wash your face. Now wash your hands. That's right, rub hard."

He will also enjoy a measure of success in pulling off his own socks and slippers. Exaggerate the pulling motion when you do it. If you make it a game and encourage him, he will try. Later, he may give serious attention to removing his shoes and socks at times which are not always convenient for you. Be accepting of these early efforts at independence, in spite of your momentary irritation.

Early practice in self-feeding encourages independence, an interest in food, and the development of eye/hand coordination. Finger food is fine for a start, but let him handle a spoon, too. Do not let the "mess" bother you. There will be some messes while your child is learning how to handle a spoon.

SUPPLEMENTARY MATERIALS OR ACTIVITIES OF MY OWN

_____

_____

RECOMMENDED TOYS

Comb and brush set (Baby World, Plakie, or Stahlwood)

8

REFINING TARGET EXPERIENCES

Dropping small objects into a plastic bottle and block building were eye/hand coordination experiences which prepared your child for ready success at this level. Beginning with the spindle game, he is introduced to circular, square and triangular shapes which he fits on a spindle in any sequence. The child experiments further with hidden objects as he retrieves the ball after dropping it into a drum. In Activity 3, success with the pegboard requires that the child exert more force and better eye/hand coordination.

Parallel Language Development. Toward the end of the first year, begin to name and point to as many familiar objects as your child appears interested in. Don't be discouraged if he doesn't repeat the words. Learning language through imitation doesn't occur until much later. And remember: babies understand the meaning of many words long before they are able to use them.

ACTIVITY 1: Shapes on the Spindle

Learning Operation: Refining eye/hand coordination to fit shapes on a spindle.

Materials: Creative blocks (Fisher-Price)

Presentation:

Demonstration. Sit with your child at a small table or on the floor. Hold the spindle in one hand and a plastic shape in the other. Randomly pick any shape but be certain to name the shape you have chosen, that is circle, square or triangle. Slowly demonstrate how you slip the shape on and down the shaft of the spindle. Say, "See, I put the circle on. Now it's your turn."

Guided Practice. At first, hold the spindle for your infant and hand him a shape. Say, "I will hold the spindle. You put the circle on."

Guide the spindle so you are pointing the end of it in his direction. He will surely be successful in hitting the target if you aim the end of the spindle as he aims the shape. Reward his effort and encourage him as he makes contact by saying, "Good! You put the circle on! Let's try again."

Independent Practice. When your guiding of the spindle is no longer necessary, place a square shape on the table and insert the spindle. Now he is ready to try to hit the target on his own. If he fails, come to his assistance and hold the base. Soon his success will be its own reward, and he will enjoy playing the spindle game by himself.

OBSERVING PROGRESS

Does the infant have difficulty fitting a shape on the spindle when you hold the spindle and guide it for him?

☐ yes   ☐ no

If yes, provide more target practice with the clothespin and bottle game and its variations.

Does he stick with the game and succeed when the spindle is placed in the square and resting on the table?

☐ yes   ☐ no

If not, help him by guiding his hand at first and holding the base securely.

Does he attempt to repeat any of the key words you have provided during this activity?

☐ yes   ☐ no

If not, continue to repeat a small number of words at the appropriate times.

If yes, show your delight in his early verbal efforts.

ACTIONS OR RESPONSES I WOULD LIKE TO REMEMBER

_____

_____

_____

TEST OF MASTERY: Given the plastic shapes, the child independently picks up and fits each shape onto the spindle.

Infant's Age in Months at Mastery _____

VARIATION: A similar homemade game may be created from the metal rings of a Mason canning jar lid and a wooden spoon. Ask him to drop the jar lid rings onto the handle as you hold the bowl of the spoon. Inexpensive plastic bracelets may be substituted for the jar rings, and a ruler may be used in place of a spoon.

SUPPLEMENTARY MATERIALS OR ACTIVITIES OF MY OWN

_____

_____

_____

_____

RECOMMENDED TOYS

Pull Train (Baby World)

Clown Stack (Playskool)

Block Stack (Sandberg)

Picky-Top (Fischerform)

Reels and Wheels (Ambi)

ACTIVITY 2: Ball in the Box

Learning Operation:

The infant uses precise eye/hand coordination and object memory to retrieve a ball he has dropped into a form box.

Materials:

Drum Drop (Playskool)

Presentation:

Demonstration. Sit with your infant at a small table or on the floor. Show him how easily you drop one of the balls into the top of the drum and then reach into the opening on the side of the drum to retrieve the ball.

Guided Practice. Attract the child's attention by showing him one of the balls. As he watches you, drop the ball through the hole in the top of the box. Ask him, "Where did the ball go?"
Encourage him to find it and express delight in his success. Now encourage him to drop the ball in the hole in the box and then to find the ball. Again, share his pleasure in the discovery and retrieval of the ball. After he has mastered these manipulations, he will enjoy playing this game independently. (Included with this toy is a barbell rod. If the toy is turned over, the rod can be used to pound a drum.)

OBSERVING PROGRESS

Does the child successfully drop the ball in the hole of the drum and retrieve it?

☐ yes ☐ no

If not, provide additional help by repeating your demonstration. You may also wish to play the hidden objects game more frequently (DEVELOPMENTAL LEVEL 4, see page 22). The early thinking skills and the recognition that an object still exists when out of sight required for success in the hidden objects game and its variations are closely related to the skills required here.

If yes, proceed to the next activity, but remember to provide many opportunities for your child to play this game. You will be surprised to observe how fascinated he is with this toy and how often he practices his new skills with it. The joy of discovery does not disappear for him, even with repetition.

ACTIONS OR RESPONSES I WOULD LIKE TO REMEMBER

_____

_____

_____

_____

TEST OF MASTERY: The child will, without hesitation, follow the necessary steps to retrieve a ball he has dropped into a form box.

Infant's Age in Months at Mastery _____

VARIATION: Your child may enjoy a simple, alternate version of this game. As he watches you, turn two paper cups upside down on the table—one of them over a small toy or block. Ask him to find the toy. He will enjoy picking up both cups even when he knows which one conceals the object. At times you may want to play this game with bite-size foods—raisins or cereal bits, for example.

SUPPLEMENTARY MATERIALS OR ACTIVITIES OF MY OWN

_____

_____

_____

_____

_____

RECOMMENDED TOYS

*Bear in the Box** (Tonka)

Jack-in-the-Music-Box (Mattel)

Pound-A-Ball (Child Guidance)

*Bear in the Box is a trademark of Tonka Toys Division of Tonka Corporation.

ACTIVITY 3: Pegs in the Board

Learning Operation: Using precise eye/hand coordination to fit large plastic pe[gs] into a rubber pegboard and to remove them.

Materials: Rubber pegboard and 25 pegs—5 each of 5 colors (Ideal)
Sorting tray or plastic bowl

Presentation:

Preview. Sit with your child at a small table or on the floo[r]. Place the rubber pegboard in front of him. Focus his attentio[n] on the holes in the board by putting your index finger in one [of] the holes and saying, "See, I can put my finger in the hole[."]
Encourage him to feel several of the holes with his finger.

Guided Practice. In the beginning, work with a supply of onl[y] five pegs of different colors which you have put in the sortin[g] tray. Demonstrate how to push one of the pegs into a hole in th[e] pegboard. Say, "See, the peg goes in a hole. Now, you put a pe[g] in a hole."

Help him push the peg down into the hole if necessary. No[w] demonstrate in a similar way how to remove a peg from th[e] board and return it to the plastic bowl. Pushing the pegs in an[d] pulling them out takes muscular force, but with help an[d] practice he will quickly learn to do both.

Independent Practice. As soon as your infant easily fits th[e] five pegs into the pegboard and pulls them out, let him wor[k] with all of the pegs which you have put in the bowl. He will, of course, always welcome your praise and encourage ment but will also enjoy playing with the pegboard by himself for relatively long periods of time.

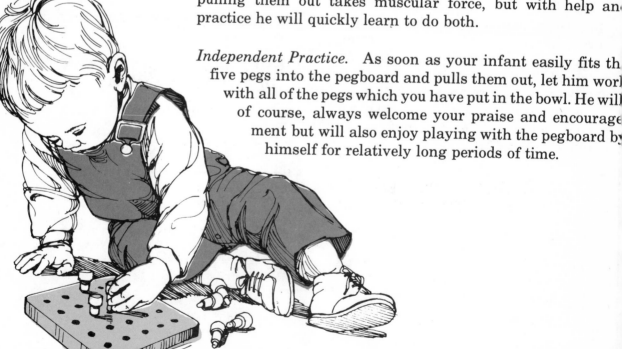

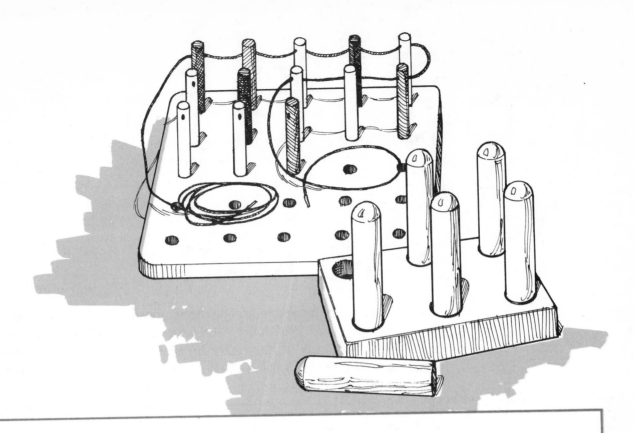

OBSERVING PROGRESS

Is the infant successful in fitting the pegs into the pegboards and pulling them out?

☐ yes ☐ no

If not, provide additional help by repeating your demonstration. Praise his efforts.

If yes, introduce color patterning as described in the VARIATION.

ACTIONS OR RESPONSES I WOULD LIKE TO REMEMBER

_____

_____

_____

_____

_____

TEST OF MASTERY: Given pegs and a pegboard, the child inserts and removes the pegs with no difficulty.

Infant's Age in Months at Mastery ———

VARIATION: After your child has mastered peg insertion and removal, encourage him to imitate color patterns you make. Insert the pegs by color; for example, make a red row or a blue row. Emphasize the color words as you play this game. To avoid confusion, you may at first want to limit the number of pegs in the tray—all the red pegs, for example, but only three or four pegs of another color.

SUPPLEMENTARY MATERIALS OR ACTIVITIES OF MY OWN

_____

_____

_____

RECOMMENDED TOYS

Jumbo Pegboard (Constructive Playthings)

Twiddle Sticks (Fischerform)

*Big—Little Pegboard** (Lauri)

Peg Play Set (Lauri)

*Big—Little Pegboard is a registered trademark of Lauri, Inc.

TAKING APART

Your infant pulls apart or separates joined parts of toys. The colorful pop beads, interlocking cubes and giant interlocking blocks require increasingly difficult pulling actions and demonstrate how the young learner is able to use the same skills acquired with one kind of material on similar kinds. At the next developmental level, he will learn that things taken apart by using a pulling motion can also be put together by using a pushing motion.

Parallel Language Development. Most children have a speaking vocabulary of 6 to 12 words between 12 and 15 months of age. And, of course, their pronunciation is far from perfect. Don't worry about this. If your child says, "Wa", for water, don't correct. Just say, "O.K., here's some water", and emphasize water as you hand him his cup. His pronunciation will improve as he continues to be exposed to the language model you provide.

ACTIVITY 1: Popping Apart

Learning
Operation: Using a pulling motion to take objects apart.

Materials: *Snap-Lock Beads* (Fisher-Price)

Presentation: *Guided Practice.* With your infant on your lap, place in his hand two pop beads which are joined together. Place one of his hands around each bead. Place your hands over his and take him through the motion of pulling the beads apart. Pull hard enough so he feels it. Say, as you pull, "Pop! We pulled them apart."

Repeat this kind of help until you feel him pulling with you. Now he is ready to try on his own.

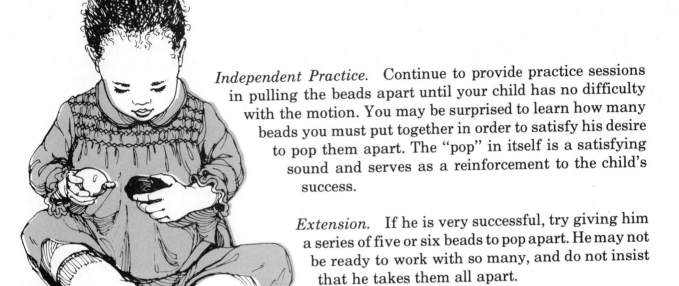

Independent Practice. Continue to provide practice sessions in pulling the beads apart until your child has no difficulty with the motion. You may be surprised to learn how many beads you must put together in order to satisfy his desire to pop them apart. The "pop" in itself is a satisfying sound and serves as a reinforcement to the child's success.

Extension. If he is very successful, try giving him a series of five or six beads to pop apart. He may not be ready to work with so many, and do not insist that he takes them all apart.

OBSERVING PROGRESS

Does the infant successfully pull two pop beads apart by himself?

☐ yes   ☐ no

If not, continue to help by placing your hands over his and taking him through the pulling motion until you feel him pulling with you. It may also help to present two accordion-shaped beads, for beads of this type offer the most rewarding "pop".

If yes, let him practice this newly acquired skill over and over again. Proceed to the next lesson which demonstrates how the child can apply what he has learned in this activity to new materials.

ACTIONS OR RESPONSES
I WOULD LIKE TO REMEMBER

_____

_____

_____

_____

TEST OF MASTERY: Given two attached pop beads, the child readily pulls them apart.

Infant's Age in Months at Mastery _____

SUPPLEMENTARY MATERIALS
OR ACTIVITIES OF MY OWN

_____

_____

_____

_____

_____

RECOMMENDED TOYS

Jumbo Snap Blocks and Beads (Stahlwood)

*Snap Mates** (Tonka)

*Snap Mates is a trademark of Tonka Toys Division of Tonka Corporation.

53

ACTIVITY 2: Separating

Learning Operation: The infant learns to take apart small, tightly fitting objects.

Materials: *Snap-Cube Builder* (Lakeshore)

Presentation:

Guided Discovery. With your infant on your lap, place in his hands two cubes which you have joined together. Place one of his hands around each cube, but do not put your hands over his. The cubes are smaller and more difficult for him to grasp than the pop beads, but give him the opportunity to discover for himself that he can pull them apart. If he shows no interest in separating the cubes, place your hands over his and take him through the motion of pulling the cubes apart. Repeat until he begins to pull with you.

Independent Practice. Provide many opportunities for him to practice this pulling apart activity. The cubes provide no satisfying "pop" as a reinforcement to success, but you can easily encourage your child to keep trying with your praise and enthusiasm.

Extension. If he is very successful, put together a rod made from four or five cubes and offer it to him. He may enjoy the challenge of taking apart a larger object; however, do not insist that he pull apart this many cubes.

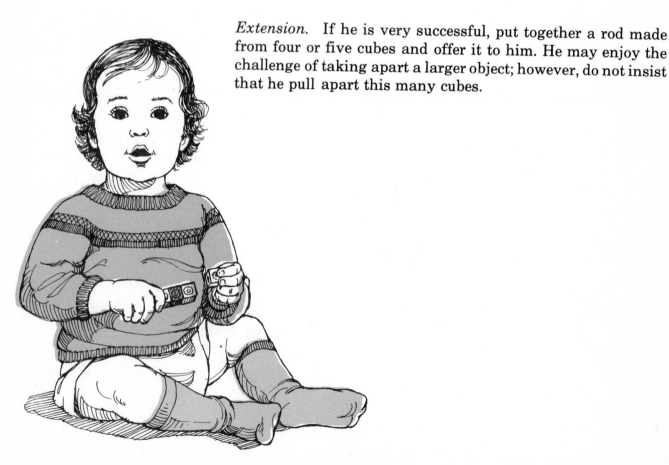

OBSERVING PROGRESS

Is the infant able to pull apart two cubes by himself on his first try?

☐ yes ☐ no

If not, continue to help him by placing your hands over his until he grasps the cubes snugly and gives a firm tug.

If yes, you've done a good job teaching with the pop beads. Your child has successfully used the skills he developed with the pop beads on new materials. The transfer process is critical to learning at all levels.

ACTIONS OR RESPONSES
I WOULD LIKE TO REMEMBER

_____

_____

_____

_____

TEST OF MASTERY: Given two joined cubes, the child grasps them firmly and pulls them apart without difficulty.

Infant's Age in Months at Mastery _____

SUPPLEMENTARY MATERIALS
OR ACTIVITIES OF MY OWN

_____

_____

_____

_____

_____

RECOMMENDED TOYS

Pop-n-Groove Builder (Lakeshore)

Snap-n-Link Builder (Lakeshore)

ACTIVITY 3: Unsnapping

Learning Operation:

Exerting a greater pulling force to take apart interlocked blocks

Materials:

Giant Interlocking Blocks (Lego)

Presentation:

Reviewing the Operation. With your infant on your lap, place one of his hands around each of two *Lego* blocks which are joined together. Place your hands over his, and take him through the motion so you are sure he feels it and say, "We can pull the blocks apart."

Repeat this kind of help until you feel him pulling with you. His hands will not fit as well around the *Lego* blocks as they did around the pop beads and cubes; he must learn to grasp more firmly as well as to pull.

Independent Practice. When you feel that he is firmly grasping the blocks and contributing to the pulling motion, encourage him to try it on his own. Say, "Now, YOU pull the blocks apart."

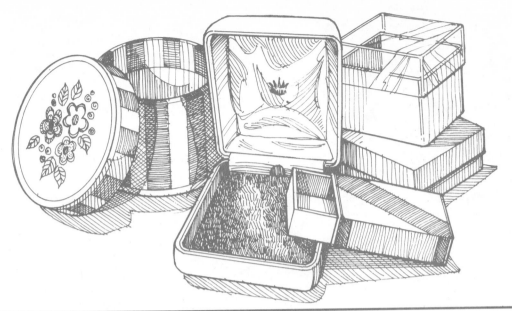

OBSERVING PROGRESS

Does the infant successfully pull the blocks apart by himself?

☐ yes ☐ no

If not, continue to help him by placing your hands over his and taking him through the pulling motion. Encourage further practice in the easier pulling operations with the pop beads and cubes, and reintroduce the interlocking blocks when he has become very skillful with the other materials.

If yes, introduce the other taking-apart activities suggested in the VARIATION.

ACTIONS OR RESPONSES I WOULD LIKE TO REMEMBER

_____

_____

_____

_____

TEST OF MASTERY: Given two interlocked blocks, the child grasps them firmly and pulls them apart without difficulty.

Infant's Age in Months at Mastery _____

VARIATION: Additional taking-apart experiences which young children enjoy include opening covers of small cardboard boxes, taking lids off pans, opening empty safety match boxes, and taking small treasures out of a drawstring bag. Occasionally, hide a surprise in one of these boxes or containers—a raisin or an animal cracker. Your baby will also enjoy pulling a brightly colored scarf out of the plastic bottle used in the target game at DEVELOPMENT LEVEL 6 (see page 34). Be sure to leave a small end of the scarf sticking out of the bottle.

SUPPLEMENTARY MATERIALS OR ACTIVITIES OF MY OWN

_____

_____

_____

_____

RECOMMENDED TOYS

*Giant Pre-School Loc Bloc** (Entex Industries)

Take-A-Part Pull Toy (Stahlwood)

*Loc Bloc is a registered trademark of Entex Industries, Inc.

Infant Developmental Level

PUTTING TOGETHER

Your child again follows a sequence of increasingly difficult actions as he joins objects by fitting and pushing together the pop beads, the interlocking cubes and the giant interlocking blocks. To complete the sequence, he must use a more forceful pushing action as well as more precise fitting skills in putting the pop beads together.

Parallel Language Development. Begin to look at simple object picture books together when your child seems interested. It could be as early as twelve months of age if he has had a lot of experience in manipulating a variety of objects. He will enjoy sitting on your lap for brief periods; helping you turn the pages. At first, connect the familiar picture object in the book with the real thing. If it's a picture of a ball, point to his ball in the room; if it's a chair, point to a real chair.

ACTIVITY 1: Pushing Together

Learning Operation:

The infant learns through experience that things taken apart with a pulling motion can also be put together with a pushing motion. He continues pushing beads together in order to make a chain of at least five pop beads.

Materials:

Snap-Lock Beads (Fisher-Price)

Presentation:

Guided Practice. With your child on your lap, place a pop bead in each of his hands. Make sure he is holding the beads so that the open end of one bead faces the knobbed end of the other. Place your hands over his and take him through the motion of pushing the beads together. Exaggerate the pushing motion so he feels it. Say as you push, "Pop! We push them together."

Repeat this kind of help until you know that he is pushing with you.

Independent Practice. Now he is ready to try on his own. Begin by handing him the beads so that the open end of one bead faces the knobbed end of the other bead. As he continues to practice, he will also examine how the beads join together. Later he will be able to pick up the beads by himself so that the open end of one faces the knobbed end of the other.

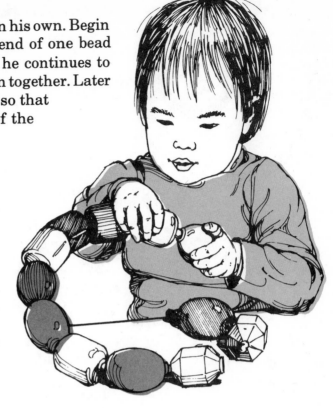

Extension. When your child can easily join two beads on his own, show him how he must move one hand up if he is to make a chain of beads. Again, do this by placing your hand over the hand he must move up and take him through the motion. Encourage him as he tries, and let him know what he is doing: "See, you must move your hand up if you want to make a LONG chain."

Share his excitement as the chain grows longer.

OBSERVING PROGRESS

Does the infant successfully join two pop beads together by himself?

☐ yes   ☐ no

If not, continue to help him by placing your hand over his and taking him through the pushing motion.

If yes, continue with this activity until he is moving his hand up and is successful in making a chain of pop beads.

**ACTIONS OR RESPONSES
I WOULD LIKE TO REMEMBER**

_____
_____
_____
_____
_____

TEST OF MASTERY: Given two pop beads, the child joins them together with a pushing motion. Given more beads, he is able to continue putting beads together until he has made a chain of at least five beads.

Infant's Age in Months at Mastery _____

**SUPPLEMENTARY MATERIALS
OR ACTIVITIES OF MY OWN**

_____
_____
_____

RECOMMENDED TOYS

Jumbo Snap Blocks and Beads (Stahlwood)

*Snap Mates (Tonka)

*Snap Mates is a trademark of Tonka Toys Division of Tonka Corporation

ACTIVITY 2: Joining Together

Learning Operation:

The infant discovers that other objects can be put together b[y] pushing and transfers his skill to new materials with greate[r] precision.

Materials:

Snap-Cube Builder (Lakeshore)

Presentation:

Guided Practice. With your baby on your lap, place a cube i[n] each of his hands so that the locking faces are opposite each other. Do not put your hands over his. Give him the opportunity to discover that he can fit the cubes together. If he does no[t] attempt to join them, place your hands over his and take him through the pushing motion. Repeat, until you feel him push with you.

Independent Practice. He is now ready to try it all by himself. Begin by handing him the cubes so that the locking faces are opposite each other, but discontinue this aid as soon as you think he can pick up the cubes by himself as well as join them.

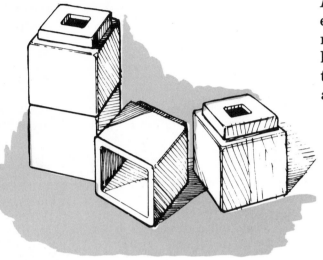

Extension: When he joins two cubes with ease, give him several more cubes. If he does not attempt to lengthen his rod, show him how he must again move one hand up in order to add another cube. Encourage him to make a rod four or five cubes in length.

OBSERVING PROGRESS

Does the infant successfully join two cubes together by himself?

☐ yes   ☐ no

If not, continue to help him by placing your hands over his until he grasps the cubes snugly and gives a firm push. You may also wish to offer more practice joining pop beads, a similar but easier operation.

If yes, share his pride in successfully applying his fitting and pushing skills to new materials. Continue presenting the activity on following days until he is joining cubes consecutively to make a longer rod.

ACTIONS OR RESPONSES I WOULD LIKE TO REMEMBER

_____

_____

_____

TEST OF MASTERY: Given two cubes, the child grasps them firmly and joins them together without difficulty. Given more cubes, he works at the activity until he has made a rod at least five cubes in length.

Infant's Age in Months at Mastery _____

SUPPLEMENTARY MATERIALS OR ACTIVITIES OF MY OWN

_____

_____

_____

_____

RECOMMENDED TOYS

Pop-n-Groove Builder (Lakeshore)

Snap-n-Link Builder (Lakeshore)

ACTIVITY 3: Fitting Together

Learning Operation: The child fits together the interlocking faces of two blocks so that he can lock them by pushing.

Materials: *Giant Interlocking Blocks* (Lego)

Presentation: *Guided Practice.* With your baby on your lap, place a block in each of his hands. Place your hands over his and line up the interlocking faces of the two blocks so that the notches match. Join by pushing. Repeat this kind of help until you think he can be successful on his own. Encourage him to examine the faces of the interlocking blocks and to feel the notches with his finger

Independent Practice. Praise him as he fits and locks two blocks together by saying, "Good! You can do it all by yourself."

Extension. Once the child understands the necessity of lining the blocks up so that the notches match, he will be immediately successful in joining additional blocks. Supply more blocks and say, "Let's make a larger building."

OBSERVING PROGRESS

Does the infant successfully fit together two blocks so that he can lock them by pushing?

☐ yes ☐ no

If not, continue to place your hands over his and guide him through the operation. If he continues to have difficulty, provide further practice in the easier joining operations with the pop beads and cubes. Reintroduce the blocks when he is able to put together the simpler materials completely on his own.

If yes, encourage him to use all the blocks to make a large building.

ACTIONS OR RESPONSES I WOULD LIKE TO REMEMBER

_____
_____
_____
_____
_____

TEST OF MASTERY:
Given two interlocking blocks, the child lines up the interlocking faces so that he can join the two blocks together by pushing. Given more blocks he will continue to make a building of at least four blocks.

Infant's Age in Months at Mastery _____

SUPPLEMENTARY MATERIALS OR ACTIVITIES OF MY OWN

_____
_____
_____

RECOMMENDED TOYS

_Giant Preschool Loc Bloc_* (Entex Industries)

Kiddie Links (Playskool)

Nuts 'n' Bolts (Child Guidance)

Bristle Blocks (Playskool)

Daisy Chain (Kiddiecraft)

_Duplo_* Line—Family Room, Sports Car, Pony Trailer, Rock 'N' Roll Pull Toy (Lego)

_Tuff Stuff_* _Wonder Blocks_ (Mattel)

*Loc Bloc is a registered trademark of Entex Industries, Inc.
*Kiddie Links is a trademark of Playskool, Inc.
*Duplo is a trademark of Lego Systems, Inc.
*Tuff Stuff is a registered trademark of Mattel, Inc.

STRINGING AND LACING

Your child has now entered the stage where he will refine the targe skills and manipulative actions he has learned through the precedin, infant activities. In the first activity of the toddler level, your child wi. learn to thread a block and later to pull out the cord. In bead stringing, hi finger movements will become more precise and he must master a three step sequence as he threads a bead, pulls the lace through and releases th lace so the bead slides down. Finally, you will see him adopting : continuous in-and-out threading action to lace along an outline.

Parallel Language Development. Time spent together daily look ing at a book will increase your child's love of books. Soon you will b successful in having him point to pictures of familiar objects in respons to "Where is the ball?" or "Show me the doll." If you are relaxed and you are enjoying one another's closeness, you will be surprised and de lighted as he not only points but also names familiar objects in books

ACTIVITY 1: Threading the Block

Learning Operation: The toddler refines his skill in finding a target by threading and unthreading a threading block.

Materials: *Thread-a-block* (Constructive Playthings)

Presentation: *Demonstration.* Sit with your toddler at a small table or on the floor. Slowly push the "needle" through a hole in the threading block. As you demonstrate say, "See, I push the needle through the hole. Now you try."

Guided Threading Practice. At first, guide your child's threading hand by placing your hand over his. Take his hand through the motion of pushing the needle through a hole in the block. Sit or kneel behind him so that you don't distract him from the business at hand.

Independent Practice. When your toddler demonstrates his understanding of the operation, remove your hand from his and let him practice by himself. Encourage him through your interest and praise.

Reversing the Operation. After he has pushed the needle through several holes and all of the cord has been used, show him how to unthread the cord by pushing the needle back through the sequence of holes. This is a difficult process for him to master, but if you continue to help and to praise him as he tries, he will keep trying and succeed. Your toddler will then be able to play happily with this toy for extended periods without assistance.

OBSERVING PROGRESS

Does the toddler, without assistance, get the needle through a hole in the threading block?

☐ yes ☐ no

If not, continue to help him by guiding his threading hand.

If yes, encourage him to continue threading the holes until all of the cord has been used.

Does the toddler remove the cord by reversing the threading operation?

☐ yes ☐ no

If not, continue to help him by guiding his threading hand back through the sequence of holes he has threaded. It may only be necessary for you to indicate to him which hole must be unthreaded next.

If yes, encourage him to play on his own with the threading block.

ACTIONS OR RESPONSES I WOULD LIKE TO REMEMBER

_____

_____

_____

_____

_____

TEST OF MASTERY:
Given the threading block, the child threads the length of cord and then reverses the operation to unthread the cord without your help.

Toddler's Age in Months at Mastery _____

VARIATION:
Large threading spools can be saved or collected for your child's first stringing efforts. If you provide him with a heavy cowhide shoestring, he should experience quick success with little help.

SUPPLEMENTARY MATERIALS OR ACTIVITIES OF MY OWN

_____

_____

_____

_____

_____

RECOMMENDED TOYS

Sewing Basket (Child Guidance) is an excellent multipurpose toy which can be used not only to provide practice in mastering the threading operation, but also reintroduced at DEVELOPMENTAL LEVELS 12, 14, and 15 for practice in **Fitting Shapes, Seriation,** and **Color Matching** (pages 73, 89, 94).

ACTIVITY 2: Stringing Large Beads

Learning Operation:

The toddler masters a three-step manipulative sequence involving threading, pulling and releasing:

a. The child holds the lace with the index finger and thumb of his right hand (or his dominant hand) in order to thread a bead held in the other hand.

b. He pulls the lace through the bead with his left hand.

c. The child opens his right hand to release the lace so the bead slides down.

Materials:

Jumbo wood beads—one-inch beads in assorted colors with stringing lace (Playskool)

Sorting tray (plastic container)

Presentation:

Independent Practice. **Threading a Bead:** Sit with your toddler at a small table or on the floor. Place a handful of one-inch beads in the sorting tray within his reach. Tie a knot in one end of the lace and offer it to him, letting him decide which hand he will use as his dominant hand. Say, "Take a bead from the tray."

Do not talk about the colors of the beads during this presentation. As soon as he has a bead in one hand and the lace in the other, encourage him to do the activity without showing him by saying, "Let's string beads. Put the lace through the hole in the bead."

If your toddler has progressed through the DEVELOPMENTAL LEVELS 1-10, he should successfully thread the bead.

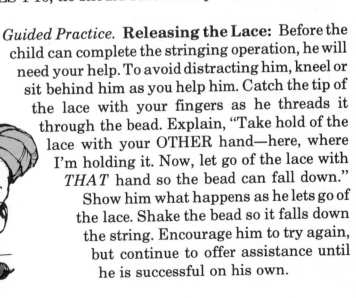

Guided Practice. **Releasing the Lace:** Before the child can complete the stringing operation, he will need your help. To avoid distracting him, kneel or sit behind him as you help him. Catch the tip of the lace with your fingers as he threads it through the bead. Explain, "Take hold of the lace with your OTHER hand—here, where I'm holding it. Now, let go of the lace with *THAT* hand so the bead can fall down." Show him what happens as he lets go of the lace. Shake the bead so it falls down the string. Encourage him to try again, but continue to offer assistance until he is successful on his own.

OBSERVING PROGRESS

Does the toddler hold the lace and thread a bead by himself?

☐ yes ☐ no

If not, provide more practice with the threading block and reintroduce bead stringing later on.

If yes, does he grasp the tip of the lace as it comes through the bead, releasing the lace with the other hand so that the bead drops down?

☐ yes ☐ no

If not, continue to catch the tip of the lace for him as he pokes it through the hole in the bead. Help him to transfer the lace from one hand to the other.

If yes, encourage him to string beads on his own. He will enjoy wearing a necklace he has made and admiring himself in a mirror. He will also be pleased if you wear a necklace of beads he has strung.

ACTIONS OR RESPONSES I WOULD LIKE TO REMEMBER

_____

_____

TEST OF MASTERY: Given a lace and a handful of one-inch beads, the toddler strings the beads by threading each bead and pulling the lace through the bead, then releasing the lace so the bead slides down.

Toddler's Age in Months at Mastery _____

SUPPLEMENTARY MATERIALS OR ACTIVITIES OF MY OWN

_____

_____

_____

_____

_____

RECOMMENDED TOYS

Large Wooden Beads (Milton Bradley or Ideal)

Big, Big Wood Beads (Sandberg)

CTIVITY 3: Stringing Small Beads

<dl>
<dt>Learning
Operation:</dt>
<dd>Transferring the manipulative skills acquired in stringing one-inch beads to half-inch beads.</dd>
</dl>

Learning
Operation: Transferring the manipulative skills acquired in stringing
one-inch beads to half-inch beads.

Materials: *Small wood beads* (Milton Bradley or Ideal)
Stringing lace
Sorting cup (margarine container)

Presentation: *Independent Transfer of Skill.* Place a handful of half-inch
beads in the cup and give your toddler a lace knotted at one end.
He should be able to proceed with no further help from you if he
has been successfully stringing the one-inch beads. The smaller
beads will now provide practice in finer eye/finger coordination.

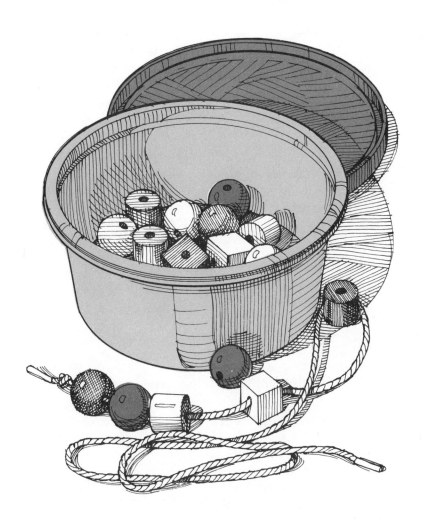

OBSERVING PROGRESS

Is the toddler successful in threading and stringing half-inch beads without your help?

☐ yes ☐ no

If not, provide more opportunities for him to use the one-inch beads rather than helping him with the half-inch beads. When he can string the larger beads with ease, he will be able to transfer this skill by himself to the smaller beads.

If yes, maintain your child's interest in stringing activities by following the suggestions given in the VARIATIONS.

ACTIONS OR RESPONSES I WOULD LIKE TO REMEMBER

_____

_____

_____

_____

_____

TEST OF MASTERY: Given a lace and handful of half-inch beads, the toddler threads the beads without assistance.

Toddler's Age in Months at Mastery _____

VARIATIONS

Stringing Two Sizes: After your toddler is successful with the half-inch beads, provide a new experience by mixing one-inch beads with half-inch beads in the same cup. Stringing beads of two sizes at random will help him both see and feel the size differences. Repeat the phrases "big bead" and "little bead" from time to time as he is handling the corresponding bead and as you admire his handiwork. Your toddler may of his own accord select only beads of one size from the mixed beads in the cup to use in a given necklace. If he makes such a choice, be enthusiastic in your response! "Oh look! You have made a necklace with only the LITTLE beads. Isn't it pretty? All the BIG beads are still in the cup."

Do not, however, insist that he string beads based on the size. Remember, at this developmental level, you are primarily concerned that he acquire the fine-motor skills necessary for stringing beads with genuine ease and pleasure, and that he experience the sense of pride and satisfaction which comes from creating a recognizable end product—the chain of beads. He will enjoy finding new uses for his products from time to time; his teddy bear or dolly, for instance, might "enjoy" wearing a necklace.

Stringing Other Objects: You might like to begin a collection of everyday household materials with "eyes" or holes which can be used for threading. Keep these in an empty three-pound coffee tin with a plastic lid. Good items for this collection include empty spools, old keys, screws with eyes, very large buttons, measuring spoons with holes in the handles, and rubber, plastic or metal washers. You will, of course, discover other interesting items to add to this assortment. Your toddler will enjoy stringing these items while improving his manipulative skills. Also, his sense of touch will become more sensitive as he handles items with unusual shapes and surfaces. The jingling noises made by some of them will also be a source of pleasure.

SUPPLEMENTARY MATERIALS OR ACTIVITIES OF MY OWN

_____

_____

_____

_____

ACTIVITY 4: Lacing Cards

Learning Operation:

The toddler threads the lace in-and-out along an outline and reverses the operation to unthread the lace.

Materials:

4 lacing cards: a line, a circle, a square, a picture
Stringing laces

Presentation:

Preparation. To make the lacing cards, use white posterboard cut in 8″ squares. Use hole puncher to form a line, a circle, a square, and simple picture—punch holes 1″ apart.

Preview. Identify and talk about the pictures on the card. Encourage your toddler to trace around the outline with his index finger and to feel the holes.

Guided Lacing Practice. Tie a knot in one end of the lace and bring it through one of the holes so that the knot is tied on the wrong side of the card. Give your child the lace in whichever hand he prefers as his dominant hand and the card in the other hand, saying, "Let's lace along the line."
Guide his stringing until he understands that he should lace through the holes in order along the line and that he must come through the holes alternately from the front and back of the card. It may only be necessary for you to indicate by pointing to the hole which comes next, saying, "Now, can you lace through this hole?"
Encourage him to choose by himself which hole comes next.

Reversing the Operation. After your toddler has become good at lacing in-and-out along the outline, demonstrate how to remove the lace. Describe the process as you perform it. "See how SHORT the string is now? Let's see how we unlace the line. There's the LAST hole you went through. I'll pull the string out of that hole. See, the string is a little longer. There's the next hole. YOU pull the string out of that hole. Good! Where's the next hole?"
Continue to point out that the string is getting longer so that the child feels there is a reward for his work.

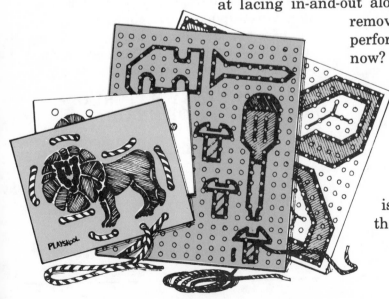

Extension. Gradually extend the lacing operation by introducing the circle, then the square and finally the picture. Be sure to name the shape as your toddler laces the card, saying, "You're doing a nice job lacing that CIRCLE."

OBSERVING PROGRESS

Does the toddler successfully lace in-and-out along the outline without your assistance?

☐ yes   ☐ no

If not, have the child use the threading block and do the bead stringing activities. Reintroduce the lacing cards later and continue to help him through demonstration and praise.

If yes, have the toddler remove the lace by reversing the operation.

Does the toddler unlace the card without assistance?

☐ yes   ☐ no

If not, continue to help him, making clear by your enthusiasm that it is as much fun to unlace the card and watch the string get longer as it was to lace along the outline of the shapes. Sometimes a toddler may resist learning to remove the lace—perhaps because of the amount of effort that was involved in lacing or because he wants to keep his work to admire or to show to another family member—and he may be genuinely upset if you insist on removing the lace. If this is the case, help him to remove the lace on another day when you can emphasize what fun it will be to make the picture again.

If yes, provide additional practice and new learning experiences as suggested in the VARIATIONS.

ACTIONS OR RESPONSES I WOULD LIKE TO REMEMBER

_____

_____

TEST OF MASTERY: Given the lace and the lacing card, the child follows the outlines with a continuous in-and-out lacing action and reverses the operation in order to unthread the lace.

Toddler's Age in Months at Mastery _____

VARIATIONS

Lacing Shoes: Although your toddler is now ready to master shoe lacing, he will enjoy being given a shoe with laces as a toy for independent play. He will spend considerable time pulling out the lace and threading it back—in a rather random fashion, of course. He may be happy with one of his old baby shoes, but he will be particularly delighted with a grownup's shoe. The eyelets are larger in an adult shoe which makes the lacing task easier.

Lacing Objects: If your child has responded with enthusiasm to these lacing activities, he will be pleased if you use the shape outlines to create simple pictures. Prepare a set of eight-inch cards which include two or three circles, squares or triangles. After you have punched along the outlines of these shapes, add details with crayons or paints to make simple objects. Do not punch along the lines you add, but along the outline of the shape. The circles can become, for example, a child's or bunny's face, a balloon, a lollipop, a clock; the squares can become a box (a bow makes it a gift), a house, a book; the triangle can become an evergreen tree or a spinning top.

SUPPLEMENTARY MATERIALS OR ACTIVITIES OF MY OWN

_____

_____

RECOMMENDED TOYS

Lacing Cards (Western Publishing)

Lacing Shapes (Lauri)

12

FITTING WHOLE SHAPES

Now your toddler will enjoy problem solving. He learns to distinguish difference in shapes while fitting them into puzzle forms, at first matching the shapes to the form by trial-and-error and then by examining the piece. Fitting the cylinder and cube into the form box should be easy if he has completed DEVELOPMENTAL LEVELS 1-10. The unfamiliar shapes provide a greater challenge, but their novelty helps to make these toys favorites with toddlers. The form board extends your child's skill in fitting shapes and introduces the concept of size. In the object puzzles, he fits simple, whole shapes into a wooden inlay board.

Parallel Language Development. As your toddler routinely imitates the names you supply for familiar objects, start to connect an action word with the name. Say, "The baby eats", or "The dog barks."

Emphasize action words in picture books. Any of the Golden Shape Books (Western Publishing) are satisfactory at this stage of development. Don't forget to carry action words into everyday activities, too. Make an effort to introduce the vocabulary of shape and size—big and little—as your child manipulates the materials in this unit.

ACTIVITY 1: Shapes in a Box

Learning Operation:

Fitting three shapes (cylinder, cube, and thin square) into their corresponding holes in a form box.

Materials:

Baby's First Blocks (Fisher-Price)
Three shapes (cylinder, cube, square)

Presentation:

Preparation. Your toddler will more easily succeed in this activity if at first you present only the cylinder shape. You may keep it hidden in your hand while your toddler explores the form box.

Preview. Let your toddler examine the form box. Point out the holes in the cover of the box and encourage him to poke a finger into these holes. Help him to open the cover and look inside. Remark that the inside of the box is empty.

Demonstration. **Introducing the Cylinder:** Show the toddler the cylinder shape. Now hold it so that a round end of the cylinder is in position to be dropped through the appropriate hole in the box. Demonstrate how by trial and error you find the corresponding hole. Then place the round end of the cylinder in the hole and drop it through. Ask your toddler to lift the cover of the box and get the cylinder. Use the word cylinder to refer to this shape, but do not expect your toddler to repeat the word. Refer to the corresponding hole in the form box as a round hole or as a circle. A cylinder can and does fit into a circular opening.

Independent Fitting Practice. Say, "Now you find the round hole for the cylinder."
    If he tries to find the correct hole by trial and error, do not intervene unless he is unsuccessful. If he fails, help him before he gives up or loses interest. Guide his index finger around the end of the cylinder and then around the corresponding hole in the form box. Emphasize that the finger feels a circle. Now let him try again.

Introducing the Other Shapes. After your toddler independently finds the correct opening for the cylinder without going through the trial-and-error process, introduce the cube. If he masters the insertion of the cylinder and the cube with ease, add the thin square. Encourage him to examine each new shape and then the holes in the form box before attempting to fit the shape. In other words, he should now begin to bypass the trial-and-error step, but do not be discouraged if he continues to rely on trial-and-error fitting rather than examination.

OBSERVING PROGRESS

Does the toddler successfully find the hole for the cylinder by the examining method instead of by trial and error?

☐ yes   ☐ no

If not, reinforce the examining method by guiding his finger around and around the end of the cylinder and around the corresponding hole in the form box. Do not introduce new shapes until he drops the cylinder in the correct hole without hesitation.

If yes, introduce the other shapes, one at a time, in their specified order.

Is the toddler successful in fitting the three shapes into their corresponding holes?

☐ yes   ☐ no

If not, drop back to the cylinder which he can fit readily and gradually reintroduce the other shapes.

If yes, encourage him to play independently with this toy.

Do not be concerned when your toddler drops back to the trial-and-error method occasionally, even after you were quite certain he had mastered the examining method. Many youngsters enjoy attempting a task they know is impossible—there's a curious pleasure in trying to fit a round peg into a square hole when you have the smug and secret knowledge that it won't go. Also, the young learner may want to reassure himself that things have remained the same—it still doesn't fit! Through trial-and-error attempts at fitting a shape into a hole, the child experiences tactile learning through the physical resistance he encounters when trying to fit a shape into the wrong hole and the ease with which a shape slips into the appropriate opening. The examining method, on the other hand, reinforces visual perception and abstract cognition. Both methods are essential to learning at all levels.

ACTIONS OR RESPONSES I WOULD LIKE TO REMEMBER

_____

_____

_____

TEST OF MASTERY: Given the form box and the three shapes, the child easily drops each shape into its appropriate opening without error and without assistance.

Toddler's Age in Months at Mastery _____

SUPPLEMENTARY MATERIALS OR ACTIVITIES OF MY OWN

_____

_____

_____

RECOMMENDED TOYS

Shape Sorter—4 shapes (Fisher-Price)

Teddy Bear Shape Sorter—6 shapes (Playskool)

Postal Station—5 shapes (Playskool)

Form Fitter—18 shapes (Child Guidance)

Sorting Box—3 shapes (Fischerform)

Posting Cube—6 shapes (Kiddiecraft)

Shape Sorter, A Nest of Rockin' Robins (Kenner)

ACTIVITY 2: Shapes and Sizes

Learning Operation:

Fitting circles, squares and triangles of four sizes into a form board and responding to the size and shape words—*big, little, middle-size,* and *circle, square, triangle.*

Materials:

Shapes and forms; wooden inset boards with shapes—4 circles, 4 squares, 4 triangles (Constructive Playthings); sorting cup (margarine container)

Presentation:

Preview. Put all the shapes into a sorting cup and present only the inset board to your toddler. Encourage him to examine it and to feel the openings with his fingers.

Guided Fitting Practice. Introduce only the biggest circle, square and triangle initially. Hand the child the circle and ask, "Where does this circle go?"

He may use either the trial-and-error method or the examining method to find the opening for the circle. Praise his achievement and present the square and triangle in turn.

Guided Practice—Big and Little. Keep the three biggest circles in place in the inset board and introduce the smallest circle, square and triangle by handing the child the circle and saying, "Here is a LITTLE circle. Where does it go?"

When he places the circle successfully, present the square and the triangle in the same manner.

Encourage him to look at the shapes he has correctly placed in the inset board. Focus his attention on the difference in size by pointing as you say, "Here is a BIG circle. This circle is LITTLE."

Repeat similar observations for the other shapes. Change the wording of your observation and speak naturally. "That's a BIG triangle. Where's the LITTLE one?"

Depending upon the language development of your child, you may choose to include other comparisons: big (bigger), large (larger), little (littler), small (smaller). Language is a flexible tool and there are many correct and acceptable ways of expressing the same observations.

Show your toddler how to turn the inset board upside down so that the shapes fall out. Help him to pick up the six shapes and return them to the sorting cup. Encourage him to put the three big and three little shapes in place again, but this time hand them to him in no special order and always with a descriptive comment: "Here's the BIG square. Where does it go? Look at this LITTLE circle. Can you find its place?"

If your toddler makes any attempt to repeat the shape or size words, respond enthusiastically. After he has replaced the six shapes, you may wish to end the lesson for the day. He may want to play by himself, however, with the inset board and the six shapes you have introduced thus far. If he remains interested, go on with the presentation. If your time is limited, complete the presentation the next day.

Guided Practice—Big, Little and Middle-Size. After the child has fit the three big and three little shapes into place on the inset board, present the remaining six shapes as the middle-sized shapes. Introduce them as you did the others. Do not be upset if your child sees a middle-size circle as little when he is comparing it to the biggest circle or as big when he is comparing it to the littlest circle. Size designations are relative words and depend on the comparison being made. The fact that the child is making his own comparisons is reason for praise, not concern.

Independent Practice. Encourage your toddler to play independently with the inset board and the shapes. He should soon be able to fit all twelve shapes into the appropriate holes by examining them with little need for trial-and-error fitting. Praise all his efforts at using shape names and size designations. Continue to repeat these words often as you observe his play and admire his completed work.

The Attribute Game. After your child can fit the twelve shapes into the board with ease and shows that he has begun to understand the vocabulary of size and shape, play this simple game of attributes. After he has completed the board, ask him to point to or to hand you a specific shape: "Give me the BIG CIRCLE. Good! Now give me the BIG SQUARE."

Change the order in which you ask for these pieces. Remember, there are two correct responses for the middle-sized pieces. Vary the game on occasion by putting away the inset board and playing only with the shapes. At first you may want to limit the pieces to only the big and little shapes in order to avoid confusion.

Responding to your requests requires real concentration from a toddler, so be generous in your praise. In verbal games such as this one, much of the reward and motivation for continuing must come from you. In contrast, when your toddler is working directly with self-corrective toys, much of the reward and motivation stems from performing the action and observing the obvious results.

OBSERVING PROGRESS

Does the toddler successfully fit all of the shapes into the inset board by himself?

☐ yes   ☐ no

If not, provide many opportunities for practice and help him learn to use the examining method rather than relying on the more tedious trial-and-error method. Encourage him to use his finger to go around and around the inset holes for the circles. How different they feel from the openings for the squares! Give him the big circle in one hand, the little one in the other. The difference in how his small hand must grasp the two circles will emphasize for him the difference in size. Some youngsters find it easier to recognize size differences when you stack the various sized shapes into sets of four, beginning with the biggest on the bottom and ending with the smallest on top.

If yes, concentrate on his response to your requests and on his own use of size and shape words.

Does the toddler respond correctly to your requests, demonstrating that he understands the shape names and size words?

☐ yes   ☐ no

If not, continue to share his play with the inset board so you can repeat these important labels at appropriate times. Continue to practice the attribute game.

If yes, reinforce size and shape words by using them whenever possible during normal household routines which involve your child. Go on to incorporate the suggestions given in the VARIATIONS.

ACTIONS OR RESPONSES I WOULD LIKE TO REMEMBER

_____

_____

_____

_____

_____

TEST OF MASTERY: Given an inset board and three shapes in four different sizes, the child easily and without help fits each shape into its appropriate place. Further, he demonstrates his understanding of the words *circle, square* and *triangle, big, little* and *middle-size* by pointing to or picking up the specific shape requested.

Toddler's Age in Months at Mastery _____

VARIATIONS

Stringing by Size: The size difference between the one-inch and half-inch beads introduced at DEVELOPMENTAL LEVEL 3 (see page 15) may become more meaningful to your toddler after he has developed further size discrimination skills

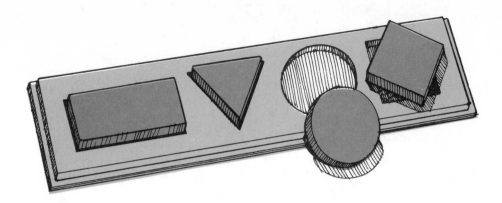

with the inset board and learned to use the labels of big and little. Help him to transfer this vocabulary to the big and little beads. He may take renewed pleasure in choosing the correct beads from an assortment of big and little beads to make a necklace of little (or big) beads. With guidance and encouragement, some youngsters are capable of making a necklace by alternating big and little beads. If your child enjoys this challenge, be sure to repeat the phrase *big bead* or *little bead* as each new bead drops down the lace.

Other Size Games: Be alert and imaginative in finding new opportunities for you and your toddler to use the vocabulary of shape and size. He can handle a big cup and a small cup, a big spoon and a little one. He can handle three sizes if you use the cups and spoons from measuring sets. If you have big and small cooking pots, your child will enjoy putting on the corresponding lids as you emphasize the appropriate size words.

Clothing can be used. Your toddler's mitten is small; Daddy's (Mommy's) is big. Let him try on the big mitten. His cap is small compared to Daddy's or an older brother's or sister's hat. Trying on the big hat is fun and a convincing demonstration of size differences. If your child enjoys looking at books with you, now is a delightful time to tell or read a simplified version of *The Three Bears*. He will enjoy hearing the familiar size words—big, little

and middle-size—in this new context. He will take a keen interest in finding these objects—the big bowl, the middle-size chair, the little bed—in the illustrations.

It is more difficult to describe objects with shape words at this developmental level, but your toddler will probably be able to succeed with the circle. His dinner plate is a circle; so are the buttons on his coat. The kitchen clock is a circle; so are the wheels on his toys.

SUPPLEMENTARY MATERIALS OR ACTIVITIES OF MY OWN

_____

_____

_____

_____

_____

RECOMMENDED TOYS

Playtiles (Playskool)

Form Board Puzzle (Playskool)

Coordination Board (Constructive Playthings)

Playpath Box and Blocks (Johnson & Johnson

Playpath Fitting Forms (Johnson & Johnson)

Geometric Sorting Board (Galt)

ACTIVITY 3: Easiest Puzzle

Learning Operation:

The toddler moves from trial-and-error fitting to the examining method in completing a four-piece puzzle.

Materials:

Four-piece *Favorite Fruits Puzzle* (Playskool)

Presentation:

Preview. Give your toddler the assembled four-piece puzzle. Point out each of the pieces—apple, banana, grapes, and pear. Show him how he can remove the pieces by turning the puzzle upside down, but turn the pieces right-side-up before encouraging him to assemble the puzzle.

Guided Practice. Let him work on his own terms as he fits the four pieces back in. If he has difficulty, you may want to position the pieces near the appropriate openings so they can be slid easily into place. At this early level, it is quite all right to help him succeed in order to keep him at the task. If he has spotted the correct opening for a piece but tries to force the piece in at the wrong angle, show him how he can turn the piece in order for it to fit.

Independent Practice. Encourage your toddler to play with the four-piece puzzle until he can assemble it easily without relying on trial-and-error manipulations. Do not, however, assume that when he can do it with ease, he will no longer be interested in doing it. Turning the puzzle over and knocking out the pieces is half the fun, and the certainty of success in reassembling builds self-confidence.

OBSERVING PROGRESS

Does the toddler fit in the four puzzle pieces?

☐ yes ☐ no

If not, offer help by positioning the pieces or by helping him to turn the pieces so they fit.

If yes, encourage him to play with the puzzle until you are sure he is relying on the examining method rather than trial-and-error manipulations. Then proceed to the nine-piece object puzzle in the next activity (page 82).

ACTIONS OR RESPONSES I WOULD LIKE TO REMEMBER

_____
_____
_____
_____
_____

TEST OF MASTERY: Given the four-piece puzzle, the child independently turns the puzzle upside down to remove the pieces and then replaces them correctly without hesitation.

Toddler's Age in Months at Mastery _____

SUPPLEMENTARY MATERIALS OR ACTIVITIES OF MY OWN

_____
_____
_____
_____

RECOMMENDED TOYS

Form Puzzles (Constructive Playthings)

First Puzzles 4 to 5 pieces (Playskool or Judy)

Puzzle 'n' Mold (Child Guidance)

Trace 'n' Play (Child Guidance)

Baby Puzzle (Stahlwood)

ACTIVITY 4: Nine-Object Puzzle

Learning Operation: The examining method is reinforced as the toddler completes a nine-object puzzle.

Materials: *Wooden inlay farm animals—puzzle with knobs (Fisher-Price)*

Presentation:

Preview. Give your toddler the assembled nine-object animal puzzle. He will be fascinated with the small knobs and will enjoy taking hold of them to remove the pieces, so do not encourage him to turn this puzzle upside down to remove the pieces. If he chooses to do so, however, do *not* restrain him; he will have many opportunities to handle the knobs. Help him to recognize and name any of the animals with which he is already familiar—the horse or pig, perhaps—but do not try to teach him animal names at this time.

Independent Practice. If your child is completely successful with the four-piece puzzle, he will probably be able to assemble much of this one on his own. Stay nearby, however, to offer encouragement and to position or turn pieces if necessary.

Elaboration. Most toddlers enjoy working this puzzle over and over again. The tiny knobs are fun to handle and offer good practice in the thumb/forefinger coordination necessary in picking up small objects. When your youngster can complete this puzzle readily, add new interest by making comments about the animals and by helping him to acquire new animal names, such as cow or duck. He will be delighted if you play an animal sound game with him as he handles these pieces. "The cow says, *'Moo-oo.'* The duck says, *'Quack-quack.''*

Your animal impersonations help to give individual puzzle pieces the quality of a toy, and your child will soon imitate some of these sounds himself. These imitations not only add to his fun but they are also an important first step in good speech development.

OBSERVING PROGRESS

Does the toddler independently and correctly fit the nine objects to complete the puzzle?

☐ yes   ☐ no

If not, help him by positioning the pieces or by turning them to make them fit. Note which animals give him difficulty. Is it the same one or two pieces which always seem to trouble him? If so, perhaps you can help him to note a distinguishing feature in the outline of the piece which will help him to make a correct fit more readily.

If yes, encourage him to play with the puzzle often so that he comes to rely on the examining method rather than trial-and-error manipulation to complete the puzzle.

ACTIONS OR RESPONSES I WOULD LIKE TO REMEMBER

_____

_____

_____

_____

_____

TEST OF MASTERY: Given a nine-object puzzle, the child removes the knobbed pieces without your help and then replaces them correctly without hesitation.

Toddler's Age in Months at Mastery _____

SUPPLEMENTARY MATERIALS OR ACTIVITIES OF MY OWN

_____

_____

_____

_____

RECOMMENDED TOYS

Vehicles, Nursery Rhymes, and *Animal Friends Puzzles* (Fisher-Price)

Zoo, Fruit, and *Pets Puzzles* (Lakeshore)

FITTING PARTS TO FORM A WHOLE

Your toddler begins to understand the relationship of a part to its whole as he puts together three- and six-piece puzzles of familiar figures. His success in fitting whole shapes into a puzzle at the previous developmental level keeps his interest now with these more difficult puzzles. The mental picture the child has of kitten and boy helps him to position the puzzle pieces to reconstruct a whole figure. (Observe the attention span and perseverance exhibited by your toddler as he completes puzzles at this level.)

Parallel Language Development. Take advantage of your child's interest in manipulating puzzle pieces in this unit to emphasize body parts, clothing and colors. Playfully contrast animal and human body parts and characteristics by asking him, "Do you have whiskers?"

Most youngsters at two years of age are capable of knowing and naming the basic colors and 15 to 20 body parts if parents or significant adults in their environment regularly name the colors of clothes they wear and emphasize the names of body parts during dressing and bath time.

ACTIVITY 1: Finish the Kitten

Learning Operation: Fitting together parts to form a familiar whole. The child is able to picture a familiar whole object by recognizing a part of the object. This is called visual closure.

Materials: Five-piece kitten puzzle (Lakeshore)

Presentation: *Preview.* Give your toddler the assembled puzzle of the kitten. Talk about the picture, naming the animal and perhaps making a mewing sound. Point out the head piece, the body piece, and the tail piece.

Discovery. Now let him turn the puzzle upside down to remove the pieces. Encourage him to turn the pieces right-side-up before beginning to assemble the puzzle. Let him discover how to fit the pieces together to form a kitten. You probably won't need to help by positioning or turning pieces to make them fit if he has been independently successful with the two earlier object puzzles.

Independent Practice. Help your toddler recall his mental picture as he works to fit the pieces. Say, "Where do you put the HEAD piece? That's the TAIL piece. Where does it go? Now, where does the BODY piece go?"
Be sure to praise the successful placement of each piece.

Provide frequent opportunities for your child to complete the kitten puzzle. Emphasize the words *kitten, head, tail, legs,* and *body.* He may also enjoy pointing to other body parts in the completed puzzle: "Where is the kitten's eye? Find its ear. Can you find its paw (foot)? Show me another paw. Where is its mouth?"

OBSERVING PROGRESS

Is the toddler successful in fitting the five-piece puzzle together without your help?

☐ yes ☐ no

If not, offer help by identifying the puzzle pieces by name—*head, tail, legs,* and *body.* If he still has difficulty, offer more practice with the four- and nine-object puzzles at DEVELOPMENTAL LEVEL 12 (see page 73).

If yes, encourage language elaboration and follow the suggestions given in the VARIATIONS.

ACTIONS OR RESPONSES I WOULD LIKE TO REMEMBER

_____

_____

_____

TEST OF MASTERY: Given the five-piece kitten puzzle, the child turns it upside down to remove the pieces and then completes the puzzle without assistance.

Toddler's Age in Months at Mastery _____

VARIATIONS

Double Puzzle Game. If your toddler is very successful with the animal puzzle, he may enjoy this surprise problem-solving game. Empty the four pieces from the favorite fruits puzzle and the five pieces from the kitten puzzle into the same sorting tray. Give him the two empty puzzle frames and the tray. Observe what he does. He may respond with delight to this new challenge and complete each puzzle readily. Some toddlers are so self-confident that they will work on the two puzzles simultaneously! If your child seems upset or confused, however, offer immediate help. Hand him the kitten pieces and put aside the favorite fruits frame. After he has completed the kitten puzzle, he can then put together the other puzzle.

Making Object Puzzles. If you wish to provide further practice in recognizing familiar wholes from their parts or if your toddler particularly enjoys puzzles, you can make simple two-piece puzzles as follows: Cut several bold, uncomplicated object pictures which you know will have appeal to your youngster. Paste each picture on a cardboard rectangle and cut it into half along any line—horizontal, vertical or a simple zigzag. (Do *not* cut it into more than two pieces because cardboard puzzles are difficult for toddlers to manipulate.) Your youngster will enjoy putting these together with you while sitting on the floor or at a low table. Encourage language association whenever possible.

Naming Game. You can play an even simpler version of this recognition-by-parts game if you and your child enjoy looking at magazines and picture books together and if he is able to name familiar objects. Occasionally use your hand or a square of paper on a picture with which he is familiar—a puppy or a kitten, for example—and ask him to name the object. Does he say *kitty* when he sees only the bottom half of the kitten? Can he recognize the dog from the tail half as well as from the front half? Being able to mentally picture a whole object when only shown a part of it is an important learning skill fostered by this as well as by all picture puzzle activities.

SUPPLEMENTARY MATERIALS OR ACTIVITIES OF MY OWN

_____

_____

_____

RECOMMENDED TOYS

Robin, Butterfly, and *Tree Puzzles* (Judy)

Duck, Horse, and *Squirrel* (Easy Puzzles) (Playskool)

ACTIVITY 2: Finish the Child

Learning Operation: The child learns to recognize and to form a familiar whole from smaller parts and to name body parts and clothing items.

Materials: Six-piece Boy or Girl Puzzle (Lakeshore)

Presentation: *Preview.* Give your toddler the assembled six-piece puzzle of the child. Talk about the picture, pointing to the body parts he knows and naming them. If your toddler has completed DEVELOPMENTAL LEVELS 1-10, focus attention on the face—a key puzzle piece in recognizing the figure as a person—by pointing to and naming the eyes, mouth, hair and ears.

Independent Learning. Encourage him to do this puzzle all by himself. He should, by now, take out the puzzle pieces with no help from you. He is also unlikely to need positioning or turning help except for one or two of the more difficult pieces. Provide many opportunities for him to work this puzzle and continue to emphasize related words. Ask your child to point to the shoes in the puzzle. Then say, "Good! Now can you show me where his eyes are?"

You can strengthen this learning by asking him to show you his own body parts or clothing items which are the same as those shown on the puzzle.

OBSERVING PROGRESS

Is the toddler successful in fitting the six-piece puzzle together without your help?

☐ yes ☐ no

If not, offer help in identifying key puzzle pieces—the face at the top of the puzzle, the shoes at the bottom, and so on. If your toddler continues to have difficulty, offer more practice with the simple object puzzles at DEVELOPMENTAL LEVEL 12 (see page 73) and with the three-piece kitten puzzle in the previous activity.

If yes, encourage language elaboration when you have time, but continue to provide opportunities for your toddler to work by himself on this puzzle. Puzzles are excellent toys for independent play because the end product of the toddler's efforts is visible and satisfying. The concentrated effort and perseverance which puzzles demand help to extend the young child's attention span, and an increased span of attention is necessary for more complicated learning activities.

You may wish to add to your child's puzzle collection by purchasing other puzzles as suggested in the VARIATION.

ACTIONS OR RESPONSES
I WOULD LIKE TO REMEMBER

TEST OF MASTERY: Given the six-piece puzzle of the child, the toddler turns it upside down to remove the pieces and then completes the puzzle without assistance.

Toddler's Age in Months at Mastery _____

VARIATION

There are many three- to nine-piece puzzles available commercially which your toddler will enjoy. Choose puzzles having picture objects with which he is familiar and ones which have language associations that he will enjoy. Other animals—a cow or horse or bird—and vehicles are usually well received by young children.

SUPPLEMENTARY MATERIALS
AND ACTIVITIES OF MY OWN

Toddler Developmental Level 14

SERIATION

Your toddler becomes more aware of size relationships and is able to act on that information. You will recall that you introduced him to the concept of size at DEVELOPMENTAL LEVEL 12 (page 73) with the shape inset board. With that particular board, shape and color were helpful cues to ensure his success. The materials in this Developmental Level offer no color cues. However, your child's success with the rings and spindle in Activity 1 is guided by the cone shaped spindle. In Activity 2, your toddler transfers his skill in stacking objects according to size from the spindle toy to graduated boxes. He will enjoy copying the way you stack, nest and hide the boxes.

Parallel Language Development. Language reinforcement during these activities is extremely important. Your child will understand the size-related words and the positional words *on, in* and *under* only if you reinforce them in your teaching. Since the concept of size is relative to each situation, do not expect your child to use size-related words in his talk as easily as he does colors or shapes. But he can begin to experience the dimensions of size through the activities in this unit and that is important.

ACTIVITY 1: Rings on a Spindle

Learning Operation: Through trial and error the child learns to fit eight rings of various sizes on a cone shaped spindle in order from biggest to smallest.

Materials: *Rock-A-Stack*—graduated plastic spindle on a base with eight graduated plastic rings (Fisher-Price)

Presentation: *Cued Discovery.* In order to ensure your toddler's success in his first attempt at putting the rings on in order, place the empty spindle in front of him and line up the rings next to the spindle according to size, biggest to smallest. Place the biggest ring so that it is next to the hand he uses most. Now the rings will be in order as he picks them up and fits them on the spindle.

Language Reinforcement. Repeat often the words which describe the order in which he places the rings of different sizes. "The BIGGEST ring goes on first. See how it fits. Which ring goes on next? Yes, it's a little bit smaller. The littlest ring goes on last."

Use all of the comparative forms—*big, bigger, biggest; large, larger, largest; little, littler, littlest;* and *small, smaller, smallest,* even though you do not expect your toddler to repeat them all. He may master *big* and *little* and *biggest* and *littlest* rather quickly however.

Guided Seriation Practice. When your child begins to enjoy fitting on the rings in order and completes the task easily, do not prearrange the rings. Mix them up and let him experiment on his own. When he tries to fit a wrong ring onto the spindle, do not say, "No-no." Rather, point to the correct ring and say, "Try that one. That's right! Now you've got it."

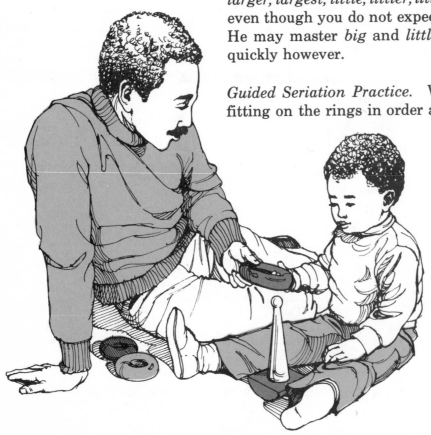

OBSERVING PROGRESS

Does the toddler correctly fit the eight rings on the spindle when you have lined up the rings by size in front of him?

☐ yes   ☐ no

If not, hand him the rings in order beginning with the biggest so that he does experience success.

If yes, allow the child to choose the correct ring from the assortment by himself. Do not line up the rings in size order for him.

Does the toddler choose the correct ring and fit it on the spindle, continuing until the eight rings have been placed according to size?

☐ yes   ☐ no

If not, continue to help him by lining up the rings in order. It may also help if you give him only the three or four largest rings for his first independent experience. If he can make the correct choices from this smaller assortment, gradually add each of the smaller rings in order until he is finally able to make the correct choices from the complete assortment of eight rings.

If yes, continue to provide play opportunities with this toy until your child can assemble the rings correctly and with ease.

At this point, his delight in the sheer mastery of the toy may continue to motivate him. You may also want to provide additional experiences in working with largest to smallest as described in the VARIATION.

ACTIONS OR RESPONSES I WOULD LIKE TO REMEMBER

_____

_____

_____

TEST OF MASTERY: Given eight rings of graduated sizes and a cone shaped spindle, the child places the rings on the spindle in sequence, beginning with the largest ring.

Toddler's Age in Months at Mastery _____

VARIATION

"Nesting" Games. Your toddler can apply his skills in stacking by size to a new situation if you collect a set of three or four different sized cans. Encourage him to put the second largest can into the largest one and to proceed downward until he has placed the smallest can into the "nest" of cans. Of course, you will make certain that no sharp edges have been left on the open ends of the cans.

He will also enjoy nesting a set of measuring cups. Continue to reinforce his experiences in stacking by size with the appropriate size-related words. Offer two cans or cups at first.

SUPPLEMENTARY MATERIALS OR ACTIVITIES OF MY OWN

_____

_____

_____

_____

_____

RECOMMENDED TOYS

Stack-N-Rings* (Tonka)

Giant Rock-A-Stack (Fisher-Price)

Block Stack (Sandberg)

Wonder Ball (Ambi)

Ring Pyramid (Fischerform)

*Stack-N-Rings is a trademark of Tonka Toys Division of Tonka Corporation.

ACTIVITY 2: Nesting and Stacking

Learning Operation:

Stacking, nesting and hiding eight different sized boxes and learning the positional words *on, in, under.*

Materials:

Stacking and Nesting Drums (eight nesting cups, all different sizes)

Presentation:

Preview. To ensure your toddler's early success in the three operations of stacking, nesting and hiding, begin with only *two cups,* a large one and a small one. Identify the cups as the *big cup* and the *little cup.* Let your toddler examine these cups before you demonstrate the operations.

Guided Practice. Put the little cup on top of the big cup (the stacking operation), saying as you do, "I'm putting the *little* cup *on* the *big* cup."

Give him the two cups and say, "You put the little cup *on* the big cup." Praise him as he follows your directions.

Now demonstrate how to put the little cup *in* the big cup (the nesting operation), saying as you do, "I'm putting the *little* cup *in* the *big* cup."

Give your toddler the two cups and say, "You put the little cup *in* the big cup."

Finally, demonstrate how to hide the little cup *under* the big cup (the hiding operation), saying as you do, "I'm hiding the *little* cup *under* the *big* cup."

Give him the cups and say, "Now, you hide the little cup *under* the big cup."

Language Reinforcement.   Continue to use key words to define what your child is doing as he plays with the cups. Emphasize the three positional words—*in, on,* and *under*—as well as the size-related words. Remember, size is a relative concept and the same cup may be *big* in one situation, *little* in another, the *biggest* in a third situation, or *bigger than* in yet a fourth setting. Don't restrict your comments to only a few phrases. Language is a flexible tool and there are many effective ways of stating similar observations.

When your toddler chooses a wrong cup in any of the operations, do not say, "No-no." Instead, offer help by suggesting, "Try that one." Praise his correct choices and minimize his errors.

OBSERVING PROGRESS

Does the toddler successfully imitate the three operations with two cups?

☐ yes   ☐ no

If not, repeat your demonstrations. Make your movements slow and deliberate, and emphasize what you are doing by what you say.

If yes, gradually increase the number of cups as your toddler demonstrates success with the three operations at each new level.

Does the toddler successfully stack, nest and hide the complete set of eight cups?

☐ yes   ☐ no

If not, drop down to the number of cups at which he demonstrates complete success and gradually build back up again to the complete set of eight. Do not hurry this progression.

If yes, encourage your youngster to play freely with the nesting and stacking cups. Follow the further suggestions in the VARIATION.

ACTIONS OR RESPONSES I WOULD LIKE TO REMEMBER

_____

_____

_____

TEST OF MASTERY: Given a set of eight different sized cups, the toddler successfully performs the three operations of stacking, nesting and hiding the cups.

Toddler's Age in Months at Mastery _____

VARIATION

Encourage your toddler to transfer the three operations to the set of cans you made for him for the VARIATION of the preceding activity. He should be able to stack, nest and hide the cans without demonstration and with little supervision. Continue, however, to provide appropriate verbal comment as you observe and admire his work: "Yes, I see, you're putting the *littlest* can on top. What a tall tower you have made!" or "Where are all the cans? Did you hide all of them under the *biggest* can?"

SUPPLEMENTARY MATERIALS OR ACTIVITIES OF MY OWN

_____

_____

_____

RECOMMENDED TOYS

Stacking & Nesting Assortment—Cubes, Barrels, and *Eggs* (Playskool)

Kitty in the Kegs, Tipsy Teacups, and *Learning Tower* (Child Guidance)

Building Beakers (Kiddiecraft)

MATCHING

Your toddler recognizes and matches colors as he plays a lotto game and strings beads by color. His vocabulary at this developmental level probably includes between one and two hundred words. If you have been looking at picture books with him, he has had experience in relating a more abstract form—pictures—to the actual objects and can probably point to and name pictures of familiar objects. In that case, he will have no difficulty recognizing familiar objects in pictures in the lotto game and in matching pairs of identical pictures. Although he may be able to match the picture and color pairs without using their names, repeat them often throughout the activity. As soon as he knows any of these words, encourage him to supply them within the context of the games.

Parallel Language Development.   Your child's understanding of the positional words *on* and *below* will be strengthened as you use them to describe his actions in the lotto games. And, since *on, in* and *under* were emphasized in the seriation activities in DEVELOPMENTAL LEVEL 14 (page 89), you can play a simple body imitation game to expand his experience with positional words.

Using a block or a penny say, "Put the penny on top of your head.," "...behind your back.," "...inside your shoe." He will imitate your actions at first but he will understand the meaning of positional words as you continue to play the game. Also, emphasize positional words as you read books together.

ACTIVITY 1: Picture Lotto

Learning Operation: The toddler learns to recognize familiar objects in pictures and to match identical picture pairs (visual discrimination).

Materials: *Object Lotto*—6 master picture cards and 36 cover cards (Edu-cards)

Presentation: *Preview.* Place one of the master lotto cards on the table in front of your toddler. Encourage him to point to and name any objects shown on the card with which he is familiar—perhaps the cup and the ball. If there are others you think he might know but cannot name, name these for him and ask him to point to them. Do not, however, attempt to teach him the names of unfamiliar objects at this time.

Guided Matching Practice. Present the small picture cards one at a time as follows: "This is my picture of a *ball*. Where is your picture of a *ball*?"

Make sure that he looks at the small picture card you are holding and then at the master card in front of him. When he finds the matching picture on his card and points to it, cover his picture with your picture, saying, "I'm putting my picture of a ball on top of your picture of a ball. Those pictures are the same."

Continue to present the other picture cards one at a time in the same manner, but encourage him to take your card and cover the identical picture on the master board.

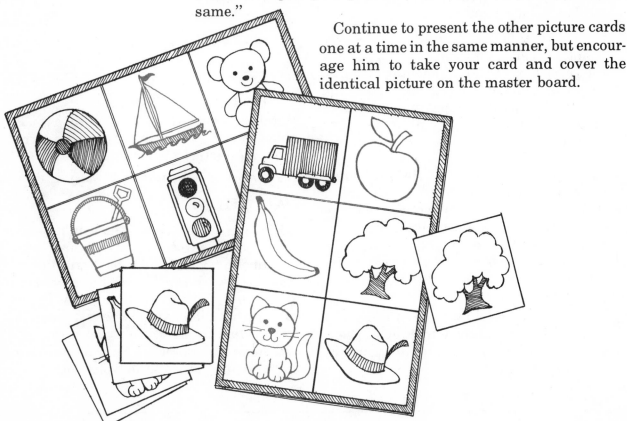

95

Language Reinforcement.   As you continue to play the picture lotto game with your child, help him to learn the names of as many of the pictured objects as possible. If, later on, he cannot initiate all these words by himself, he will probably be able to point to the correct picture after you name the object. Include the words *same (alike)* and *different* as you describe the operations connected with this game. "Those two pictures are *alike!* Here is a picture of a drum and there is a picture of a drum."

"These two pictures are *different*—this is a picture of a cup, but that is a picture of a ball?"

Independent Practice.   After your toddler has refined his matching skills, he may enjoy playing this lotto game by himself. Of course, there will be less language reinforcement when the child plays alone, but the practice in visual discrimination is important. Also, solitary play with this game demonstrates your toddler's lengthening attention span. Be pleased and proud that he is developing habits of concentration and working on hiw own.

OBSERVING PROGRESS

Does the toddler successfully match picture pairs of familiar objects in order to play the lotto game?

☐ yes   ☐ no

If not, provide additional experience with the form box at Developmental Level 12 (page 73). The examining and matching skills required to fit shapes into the correct openings in the form box build a readiness for picture matching. It will also prove helpful to look at picture books and magazines with your toddler. He will enjoy pointing to familiar objects and naming them when he can. This activity will increase his recognition and use of names and labels, foster his ability to recognize familiar objects in pictures, and generally intensify his interest in words and pictures.

If yes, encourage him to play the game often with you and sometimes by himself. Introduce the picture games described in the VARIATIONS.

ACTIONS OR RESPONSES I WOULD LIKE TO REMEMBER

_____

_____

_____

TEST OF MASTERY: The toddler matches each lotto picture card as it is given to him by placing it over the corresponding picture on the master card.

Toddler's Age in Months at Mastery _____

VARIATIONS

Picture Scrapbook: You can increase your toddler's interest in pictures and his labeling vocabulary by beginning a scrapbook with him. When he recognizes *and names* a picture in a magazine (dog), cut out that picture while he watches you and paste it in his scrapbook.

"There! You know that's a picture of a dog and you can say the word *dog.*"

Each time he provides the label for another picture (cup, kitty, baby), add that picture to his scrapbook. You will be surprised to discover how he delights in looking through his scrapbook and naming the familiar objects. He may even enjoy "reading" it by himself; that is, naming each object as he turns the pages. Of course, he will be pleased to "read" this book with another family member—Grandma, brother, uncle.

Other Picture Lotto Games: You can make your own lotto games at very little cost. If your youngster watches you make these and can handle the picture cards as fast as you produce them, his interest in the game will be intensified. He will recognize immediately that you are making these *for him.* Cut the master cards and picture cards from white cardboard ahead of time. Use the pictures from children's playing cards, from duplicate copies of sticker books or from sets of gummed seals which you can purchase at drug or discount stores. Remember, you must have *two identical* pictures of each object, one to paste on the master board and another to paste on the corresponding picture card. You can, of course, use pictures from catalogs and magazines if you have duplicate copies.

SUPPLEMENTARY MATERIALS OR ACTIVITIES OF MY OWN

_____

_____

_____

RECOMMENDED TOYS

Zoo, Farm Go-Together; What's Missing? and *ABC Picture Lotto Games* (Edu-cards)

Dolch Picture Readiness Lotto (Garrard Publishing)

Animal Dominoes (Western Publishing)

Picture Lotto (Galt)

*Zoo, Farm Go-Together; What's Missing? and ABC Picture Lotto are registered trademarks by Binney Smith Inc.

ACTIVITY 2: Color Lotto

Learning Operation:

Recognizing six basic colors and matching identical color cards—red, yellow, blue, green, purple, orange.

Materials:

1 master card and 6 matching color cards

Presentation:

Preparation. Cut two, 6″ squares of white cardboard. Divide both cards into six sections. Color each section a different color—(1) blue, (2) green, (3) red, (4) yellow, (5) orange, (6) brown. Cut out the six color sections of one of the cards. Use the uncut card as the master card.

Preview. Place the color lotto master card on the table in front of your toddler. If you know he can name a color, point to it and ask him to do so. Do *not,* however, attempt to teach him the color words at this time.

Guided Matching Practice. Present the single color cards one at a time as follows: "This is the *red* card. Where will we put it?"

Demonstrate how the color card fits on the master card. Say, "I'm putting the *red* card here, on the top of the other red space."

Continue to present the color cards one at a time, encouraging the child to take each card and place it on the matching color of the master card.

Language Reinforcement. Remember to name each color as you present the cards, but do not expect your toddler to repeat all of these at this developmental level. If he does repeat your word, *red,* for example, show your enthusiasm and encourage him to repeat the word often as you play the game and to apply it in other situations. "Yes, it's *red* like your shirt"; "It's *red* like Mommy's sweater."

Independent Practice. Play this game often with your child and encourage him to play it sometimes by himself. Remember, however, he can provide a correct color match long before he really understands the concept of color or can use color words meaningfully.

OBSERVING PROGRESS
Does the toddler successfully match the color cards and place the small card in the appropriate space on the master board?

☐ yes ☐ no

If not, repeat your demonstration.

If yes, provide the other color experiences described in the VARIATIONS.

ACTIONS OR RESPONSES
I WOULD LIKE TO REMEMBER

_____

_____

TEST OF MASTERY: The toddler matches each lotto color card as it is given to him by placing it on top of the corresponding color on the master board.

Toddler's Age in Months at Mastery _____

VARIATIONS

Color Block Lotto: Your toddler will enjoy playing another version of the color lotto game. You will need only the master card from this activity and the colored blocks introduced in DEVELOPMENT-AL LEVEL 16 (page 103).

Place the master card in front of him. Put the blocks which match the colors shown on the lotto board in one of the sorting cups. As your toddler chooses a block from the bowl and matches it to the corresponding color on the master lotto card, be sure to name the color.

Color Riddles. When your toddler begins to associate color with the color words, introduce a riddle game for a few minutes at a time after the two of you have been playing **Color Lotto.**

Hold up a color card (red) and ask him to show you something else that is red. Make this an easy task at first by giving generous hints: "Look at your socks. Yes! Your socks are red, too."

Don't overlook opportunities throughout the day to identify the colors of familiar objects: "Today you are going to wear your new *brown* shoes."

The young child enjoys relating color words to the foods he eats, to his clothing and toys, to flowers and vehicles.

Color Collections: Toddlers love surprises and miscellaneous collections of small items. Capitalize on these interests by using three-pound coffee tins as containers for small one-colored objects. Add to this collection from time to time. It might, for example, contain a green pocket comb, a blue square of felt, a yellow plastic spoon, a red scarf, an orange block, a large purple button. Encourage your child to examine the contents of the can and focus his attention on the colors as he plays: "Can you find something red? Yes, the scarf is red. Why don't you try it on? Oh dear, now you need to comb your hair. Can you find the comb? What color is the comb? Good! It's green, and you said that all by yourself."

SUPPLEMENTARY MATERIALS
OR ACTIVITIES OF MY OWN

_____

_____

RECOMMENDED TOYS
Frame Tray Puzzle Color
(Western Publishing)

ACTIVITY 3: Stringing by Color

Learning Operation:

Transferring new perceptual skills to familiar materials.

Materials:

One-inch and half-inch beads in assorted colors from DEVELOPMENTAL LEVEL 11 (pages 69)
Sorting cup (margarine container)
Stringing lace

Presentation:

Preparation and Guided Transfer of Skill. Put all of the re beads of both sizes into a sorting cup. Add beads of the othe colors, but keep a much larger number of red beads. Your toddle will enjoy applying new skills to familiar toys and discoverin possibilities. Encourage him to make a red necklace. Help hir by handing him each red bead until he begins to understan that he is matching red beads; then let him proceed on his own

Independent Practice. Your child will enjoy making necklace of other colors. Later, do not encourage him to pick a color b providing a greater number of beads of one color. Ask him wha color necklace he wants to make or let him choose a bead. "Good you picked a *green* bead. Now, let's make a green necklace.'

Remember, the young child ofter wants to keep the end product of his labor. Allow him to wear his necklace for the day—it took considerable con centration and effort for him to make it. Perhaps he would like to save it to show to Mommy o Daddy when she or he comes home—a marvelous op portunity to say tha new word *green* again!

OBSERVING PROGRESS

Does the toddler consistently choose beads of one color from an assortment of beads in order to make a one-color necklace?

☐ yes   ☐ no

If not, continue to hand him the beads, one by one, pointing out that the color is the same. Encourage him to examine his necklace as it gets longer and to note from time to time that all the beads he has strung are the same color.

If yes, urge him to make other single-color necklaces as part of his bead-stringing play.

ACTIONS OR RESPONSES I WOULD LIKE TO REMEMBER

_____

_____

_____

TEST OF MASTERY: Given an assortment of colored beads and a lace, the child chooses a bead and strings a necklace of beads which match the color of the first bead.

Toddler's Age in Months at Mastery _____

VARIATION

Finger Painting. If you don't mind the cleanup, finger painting with color can be an intense and vivid color experience for your child. If he has begun to recognize a color (red) rather consistently,

introduce *that color only* in finger painting activities. Feeling and squeezing and pushing the paint about gives a satisfying sense of red. Be sure to repeat the color name as often as he paints. Paint with the other colors one at a time as he begins to name and recognize them.

Finger paints can be made quickly and inexpensively at home by combining soap flakes, liquid laundry starch and poster paint or powdered paint. The soap flakes help in the cleanup later on. You can use a slick white shelf paper to paint on if you do not have finger-painting paper.

An even easier finger paint can be made by pouring a small puddle of liquid starch directly on the toddler's paper and merely adding a bit of paint. Let him create the color as he mixes the starch and paint by pushing it about.

SUPPLEMENTARY MATERIALS OR ACTIVITIES OF MY OWN

_____

_____

_____

_____

_____

RECOMMENDED TOYS

Stacking and Nesting Assortment (Playskool)

Nuts 'n' Bolts* (Child Guidance)

Colored Wood Blocks (Playskool)

*Nuts 'n' Bolts is a trademark of Child Guidance

16 Toddler Developmental Level

SORTING

Your toddler utilizes his matching skills when he sorts materials by color, shape, size and picture likeness. Sorting at this level is similar to matching because you provide a cue for the operation. When he sorts by color, for example, the color block you place in each sorting cup serves as a cue for him to match. The sorting operation is gradually expanded and your toddler will complete activities involving six colors, four shapes, two sizes and five picture sets.

Parallel Language Development. You will find many opportunities to reinforce your child's previous experiences with the vocabulary of shape, color and size. He will enjoy finding and naming shapes in objects he encounters every day. The top of his cup is a circle, so is his dinner plate, a doughnut, a button on his coat, a wheel on his truck. Tabletops, windows, pictures, clocks and books may be rectangles or squares. If your toddler likes to look at books and magazines with you, he may find it fun to look for shapes in these pictures. Don't search for all the shapes at the same time. It's more fun, for example, to page through a magazine with him and look only for circles.

Continue to find opportunities to compare sizes of familiar objects— big and little cooking utensils of all sorts; cans and boxes of various kinds as you unpack the groceries; big shoes, little shoes, and dolly's very, very little shoes. Most youngsters will immediately recognize the difference between a big cookie and a little cookie or a big spoon of ice cream and a little one. Remember to reread *The Three Bears* for its particular emphasis on size-related vocabulary.

ACTIVITY 1: Colors

Learning Operation: Color sorting by discriminating among six basic colors.

Materials: Cubical counting blocks in 6 colors (Milton Bradley or Ideal)
Six sorting cups (margarine containers)

Presentation: *Preparation.* At first bring to the table only the red, yellow and blue blocks and three cups. Do not distract your child by having the remaining blocks nearby.

Cueing the Operations. Place the three cups on the table in front of your toddler. Drop a red block in one container saying, "This cup is for *red* blocks."

Drop a blue block in the second container saying, "This cup is for *blue* blocks."

Drop a yellow block in the third container saying, "This cup is for *yellow* blocks."

Independent Practice. Put eight or ten red, yellow and blue blocks on the table in front of him. Say, "Put these blocks in the right cup."

As he drops each block into the correct container, provide him with the name of the color by saying, "That's a *blue* block. It goes with the other blue blocks."

Extension. Gradually extend the color-sorting operation as your toddler demonstrates that he can easily sort three colors without error. Introduce the green, orange and purple blocks—one color at a time—and supply additional cups. Soon he will be sorting six colors during the same operation and without difficulty.

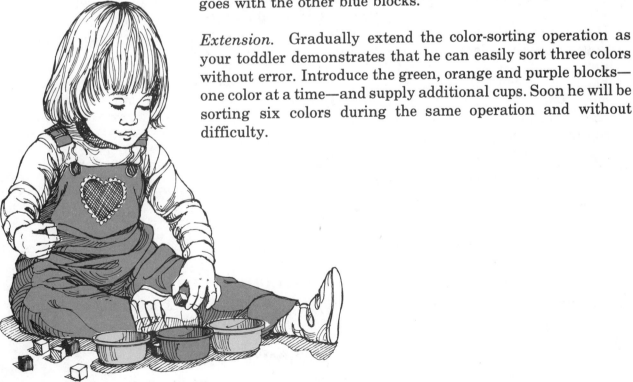

OBSERVING PROGRESS

Does the toddler sort the red, yellow and blue blocks into three cups without help?

☐ yes   ☐ no

If not, repeat your demonstration and continue to hand him the blocks to be sorted one at a time. Reinforce his color-matching skills by continuing to play **Color Lotto** and its VARIATIONS as described in DEVELOPMENTAL LEVEL 15, (pages 94-101).

If yes, add new colors to the operation until your child is sorting blocks of six colors into six cups.

Does the toddler sort blocks of six colors accurately into six cups without your help?

☐ yes   ☐ no

If not, drop back to whatever number of colors he can sort accurately and gradually build up from there by introducing new colors one at a time. Do not hurry with this progression.

If yes, continue to play this game with your toddler in order to reinforce the color names, but also permit him to sort the blocks by himself if he enjoys independence. When he attempts to use color words, show your pleasure and encourage him to repeat them in other contexts.

ACTIONS OR RESPONSES I WOULD LIKE TO REMEMBER

_____

_____

_____

_____

_____

TEST OF MASTERY: Given wooden blocks in six colors, the toddler sorts the blocks by color into six cups as part of one sorting operation.

Toddler's Age in Months at Mastery _____

VARIATION

Sorting Color Objects. For variety, combine some of the red, yellow, blue, and green teddy bear miniatures from DEVELOPMENTAL LEVEL 18 (page 126) with an assortment of blocks your toddler is about to sort by color. These miniatures are delightful to handle and will add to the fun of sorting.

On another day, add a handful of one-inch and half-inch beads in assorted colors to the teddy bear miniatures and the blocks about to be sorted. New materials make the task more interesting and also help to focus attention on the skill—sorting by color. The toddler is *not* sorting blocks—he is sorting by *color*. Teddy bears, blocks, big and little beads may go into the *same* container not because they are identical items but because they are all the same color.

SUPPLEMENTARY MATERIALS OR ACTIVITIES OF MY OWN

_____

_____

_____

_____

_____

RECOMMENDED TOYS

Scribbler's* See & Know Color Cards (Western Publishing)

*Scribbler's is a trademark of Western Publishing, Inc.

ACTIVITY 2: Shapes

Learning Operation: Distinguishing differences among four shapes in order to sort them.

Materials: Two-inch circles, squares, triangles and rectangles
Four sorting cups (margarine containers)

Presentation: *Preparation.* Cut six each of a circle, square, triangle and rectangle from white posterboard or cardboard. (Each shape should be about two inches wide.)

At first, bring only the circles, squares and triangles and three cups to the table. Do not confuse your child by introducing the unfamiliar shape—the rectangle—during this sorting operation. You will recall that he was introduced to the circle, square and triangle as an infant at DEVELOPMENTAL LEVEL 9 (page 52) and again as a toddler with the form box and the shape inset board at DEVELOPMENTAL LEVEL 12 (page 73).

Cueing the Operation. Place the three cups on the table in front of your child. Drop a circle in one of the cups saying, "The *circles* go in this cup." Drop a square in the second cup saying, "The *squares* go in this cup." Drop a triangle in the third container saying, "The *triangles* go in this cup."

Guided Sorting Practice. Begin by handling your child a circle saying, "Where does this circle go?"

If he is puzzled, point to the correct cup and say, "This cup is for the circles."

Continue to hand him shapes one at a time until he begins to place them correctly without hesitation. Praise him for his accuracy.

Individual Practice. Put eight or ten assorted shapes in front of him on the table saying, "Put these shapes into the right cup."

As he drops each shape into the correct container, provide him with the name of the shape by saying, "That's a *triangle*". "That's a *circle*". "That's a *square*".

Extension of the Operations. When your toddler successfully sorts three shapes, add the fourth cup and the rectangle. Continue to practice with him until he can sort four shapes correctly and easily.

OBSERVING PROGRESS

Does the toddler successfully sort three shapes—the circle, square and triangle—into three cups without help?

☐ yes   ☐ no

If not, repeat your demonstration and continue to hand him the shapes to be sorted one at a time. It may focus his attention on the feature of each shape if you help him to trace around it with his index finger. His finger glides easily around and around a circle but must stop and start as it turns the corners of a square and triangle. If he continues to have difficulty, offer more practice at DEVELOPMENTAL LEVEL 12 (page 73) with the form box and shape inset board. Both of these are excellent preparation for this sorting activity.

If yes, introduce the rectangle and the fourth cup.

Does the toddler successfully sort four shapes—the circle, square, triangle and rectangle—into four cups without help?

☐ yes   ☐ no

If not, provide more practice with the three shapes first introduced and reintroduce the rectangle later. Observe your toddler's errors carefully. Is he making any sorting error consistently? Does he, for example, always sort the circles and triangles correctly but confuse the squares and rectangles frequently? If so, draw his attention to the differences between these two shapes.

Stack a square and a rectangle together so he can see that their outlines do not match. Encourage him to trace around these shapes with his index finger. Even though you cannot explain these differences to your toddler in words, he can sense the four equal sides of the square and the long and short sides of the rectangle. It may also help him to identify the difference if you give him only the squares and the rectangles to sort. Remove the other two shapes from the assortment and two of the cups. Now he must focus all of his attention on one problem: the difference between a square and a rectangle. When he can successfully sort these two shapes, return the circles and the triangles to the assortment and give him four cups.

If yes, continue to play this sorting game with your toddler in order to reinforce the shape names. If he names a shape, respond with enthusiasm and encourage him to repeat the word often. Toddlers often enjoy solitary play with these shapes merely because they enjoy handling them. Encourage your youngster to manipulate the shapes freely because he will learn a great deal from the experience. Learning through touch is important to young children, and we never completely abandon that means of learning. When, as adults, we say, "Let me *see* how that works," what we really want to do is get our *hands* on the object to find out! Tactile learning is often a slow process, but what we learn that way, we never forget. Learning to ride a bicycle, for instance, is a slow and sometimes painful process, but once we have mastered that skill, we never forget how to do it.

ACTIONS OR RESPONSES
I WOULD LIKE TO REMEMBER

_____

_____

_____

_____

_____

TEST OF MASTERY: Given an assortment of circles, squares, triangles and rectangles, the child sorts them by shape into four cups without hesitation. *Toddler's Age in Months at Mastery* _____

VARIATIONS

Remember that the earlier shape toys from DEVELOPMENTAL LEVEL 12 (page 73), the form box and the shape inset board, will have new meaning and interest as your youngster's understanding of shape develops. He will now enjoy independent play with these familiar toys on new terms.

Sizes and Shapes. If your child has been *very* successful with the shape-sorting activity, you might want to introduce a new variable.

Cut an assortment of the four shapes from colored construction paper or cardboard. Include a size range for each shape. Cut, for example, circles which vary in diameter from one inch to four inches. Provide a similar range for the squares, triangles and rectangles. Be sure that you do not unintentionally provide a color cue by cutting all of the circles, for instance, from the blue cardboard and all of the triangles from yellow. Either provide assorted colors for each shape or cut all shapes from the same color. As your toddler sorts with this set, he is distinguishing among the features of four shapes, and he is also noting that circles, for example, may come in four sizes but that they are *still* circles.

SUPPLEMENTARY MATERIALS
OR ACTIVITIES OF MY OWN

_____

_____

_____

_____

_____

ACTIVITY 3: Big and Little

Learning Operation: Distinguishing between objects of two sizes in order to sort them.

Materials:

8 one-inch and 8 half-inch colored beads from
DEVELOPMENTAL LEVEL 11 (pages 67 & 69)
2 sorting cups (margarine containers)
1 sorting tray (plastic bowl)

Presentation:

Cueing the Operation. Place two cups on the table in front of your toddler. Drop a one-inch bead of any color in one cup and say, "The *big* beads go in this cup." Now drop a half-inch bead of any color in the other container and say, "The *little* beads go in this cup."

Guided Sorting Practice. Begin by handing your child a big bead saying, "Where does this big bead go?"

If he is puzzled, point to the correct cup and say, "This cup is for the *big* beads."

Continue to hand him beads one at a time, referring to each bead as big or little. Praise his successes.

Independent Practice. When he is placing the beads accurately in each cup, give him both big and little beads in the sorting tray and say, "Put these beads into the right cup."

As he drops each bead into the correct container, supply the correct size labels: "That's a *big* bead. That's a *little* bead."

Many toddlers will echo these words. If your toddler does, be enthusiastic! Encourage him to say *big* and *little* with you as the beads drop into the correct bowls. Later, encourage him to repeat the words all by himself as he continues to sort the beads.

OBSERVING PROGRESS

Does the toddler successfully sort the big and little beads into two cups without help?

☐ yes   ☐ no

If not, repeat your demonstration and continue to hand him the beads one at a time until he is sorting with accuracy.

If yes, continue to practice with him in order to reinforce the use of big and little. Encourage your youngster to repeat the words *big* and *little* and then use them on his own. Go on to provide related activities as suggested in the VARIATIONS.

ACTIONS OR RESPONSES
I WOULD LIKE TO REMEMBER

_____
_____
_____
_____

TEST OF MASTERY: Given an assortment of one-inch and half-inch wooden beads, the toddler sorts them by size into two cups without assistance.

Toddler's Age in Months at Mastery _____

VARIATIONS

Stringing by Size. Your toddler may now show more interest in bead stringing by size as was suggested earlier, in DEVELOPMENTAL LEVEL 11, Activity 2 (page 67). He may enjoy making a necklace of beads of one size as he chooses beads of the correct size from an assortment. If he is very interested in bead stringing, he may now show more interest in making a necklace of beads which alternate in size as was suggested in DEVELOPMENTAL LEVEL 11, Activity 3 (page 70).

Sorting Objects. If your toddler enjoys sorting activities, he may respond with enthusiasm to new sorting materials.

Mix together in a plastic container a handful of dried lima beans and a handful of smaller beans such as Navy beans. Give him two cups and ask him to sort the big beans into one cup and the small beans into the other. As he sorts, he will also be refining his ability to pick things up.

If you have a large collection of buttons in your sewing supplies, prepare a similar activity by choosing a dozen or so big buttons and a dozen or so little buttons. The buttons in each category must be of the same size but should not be of the same color or design. Mix them in a sorting tray and give the toddler two other cups to use for sorting.

You also can use the construction paper or cardboard shapes you prepared for the preceding activity **Shapes** (page 105). Pick out shapes in *only two* sizes with a strong contrast between *big* and *little*— the one-inch shapes and the four-inch shapes, for example. Mix these shapes in a pile and give your toddler two cups for sorting big and little shapes. Some toddlers are puzzled by this assignment and try to separate the circles from the squares—in other words, to sort by shape instead of by size. Do not allow your toddler to become frustrated. Instead, drop down to a simpler level. Give him only the big and little circles and the two cups. Now ask him to put the big circles in one cup and the little ones in another. He will have no difficulty following this request. As he is successful, he will soon be able to generalize and you may gradually add the other shapes in two sizes to the assortment. He will now use the two cups to sort four shapes according to size.

SUPPLEMENTARY MATERIALS
OR ACTIVITIES OF MY OWN

_____
_____
_____
_____

ACTIVITY 4: Picture Sets

Learning Operation: Recognizing familiar objects in pictures and sorting identical pictures into sets.

Materials: Five sets of animal pictures—4 in each set (Dennison or Hallmark)

Five sorting cups (margarine containers)

Presentation:

Preparation. Purchase a booklet of animal seals, and attach seals to 2″ squares cut from white posterboard. Choose two picture sets which you are sure your toddler can recognize. The kitten and dog may be good choices if your toddler knows these animals. Put aside the other sets of pictures to avoid confusing or distracting the child.

Preview. Show him one picture of the dog. Ask him what he sees there. Encourage him to say *dog* or a toddler's variant of the word: *dog-ee, puppy* or even *bow-wow.* Show him the picture of the kitten and see if he can name the animal.

Cueing the Operation. Place two cups on the table in front of your toddler. Drop the dog picture into one cup saying, "The dog pictures go in this cup."

Drop the kitten picture into the other container saying, "The kitten pictures go into this cup."

Guided Sorting Practice. Now hand him the remaining dog and kitten pictures one at a time, identifying each one as you give it to him: "Here is a picture of a dog. Where does it go? Here is a picture of a cat. Where does it go?"

If he hesitates, indicate the correct container saying: "The dog pictures go in this cup."

Continue to hand him the pictures until they have all been sorted. Hopefully he will be repeating the words *dog* and *kitten* or reasonable variations of the words. Praise his sorting skills and especially his verbal efforts.

Independent Practice. Empty the two cups and mix the eight pictures. Give them to the child and ask him to put the pictures of the dog and the kitten into the right cup. He should be able to do this with no help from you, and should put the dog pictures in one container and kitten pictures in the other.

Extension of the Operation. Gradually expand the picture sorting operation by introducing the remaining three sets of pictures. Do not rush this sequence, and soon your toddler will be able to accurately sort the five sets of pictures into five cups as part of one sorting operation.

OBSERVING PROGRESS

Does the toddler successfully sort the dog and kitten pictures into two cups without help?

☐ yes ☐ no

If not, continue to demonstrate the operation. Spend more time looking at the pictures with him and talking about the animals. Continue to hand him the pictures one at a time.

If yes, gradually introduce the three remaining sets into the sorting operation.

Does the toddler sort the five sets of identical pictures into five cups without help and as part of one sorting operation?

☐ yes ☐ no

If not, go back to where he is successful—two or three sets perhaps—and gradually reintroduce the remaining sets.

If yes, maintain his interest in sorting operations by doing the VARIATIONS.

ACTIONS OR RESPONSES I WOULD LIKE TO REMEMBER

_____

_____

_____

TEST OF MASTERY: Given five sets of identical pictures, the toddler sorts them into five cups without assistance and as part of one sorting operation.

Toddler's Age in Months at Mastery _____

VARIATIONS

Picture Sorting Games. You can make several sorting games by purchasing additional booklets of gummed seals. Choose subjects which will interest the child—farm animals, flowers, fish, birds, fruit. Since each booklet contains a number of identical seals, all you need do is cut more posterboard into 2″ squares and paste a seal on each square. Introduce this game to your toddler just as you presented the sets of identical animal pictures. Offer only two sets of identical pictures first and then build up to three or four. Do not ask your toddler to sort more than five sets, but do give him new combinations of picture sets to add visual interest and to foster language development.

Alphabet Sorting. If your child has enjoyed picture sorting and has been successful, you can introduce capital letters in the alphabet game.

Cut 2″ squares of white cardboard. Print a letter in the center of each square, beginning with A, and make five copies of each letter. Follow the presentation given for the picture sets. Tell your toddler, as you drop each letter into a container: "The A goes in this cup. The B goes in this cup. The C goes in this cup."

Always refer to the name of the letter as you hand him an alphabet card or as he picks one up and drops it into the correct container. Gradually add new letters. If he is truly interested in this game, you may add new combinations of letters until he has completed the alphabet. Do not, however, insist on pursuing this activity if your toddler becomes bored with letter sorting. If he completed the A, B, C sequence, try to determine whether or not he can recognize a capital A in another format—a newspaper headline, an advertisement, or in the large print of a nursery book. The ability to recognize a familiar symbol in a new situation is far more important to his learning at this level than merely sorting a large number of letters.

SUPPLEMENTARY MATERIALS OR ACTIVITIES OF MY OWN

_____

_____

RECOMMENDED TOYS

Preschool Counters
(Constructive Playthings)

Self-adhesive seals (Dennison, Hallmark)

Scribbler's* See & Know Object Cards
(Western Publishing)

*Scribbler's is a trademark of Western Publishing, Inc.

FINE MOTOR CONTROL

The toddler acquires a number of fine motor skills in order to enjoy traditional art materials: soft clay, crayons, scissors, paste and tracing forms. His interest in these materials can be encouraged by your praise and enthusiasm. It is important that he have daily opportunities to experiment by himself as well as with your help. When he masters basic skills, he will enjoy experimenting freely on his own.

Parallel Language Development. Richard Scarry's *Best Word Book Ever* is an excellent resource book for your child when he has a one- to two-hundred-word vocabulary. There are over 1400 objects, all beautifully illustrated, which will provide the stimuli for "What's that, Mommy?" or "What's that, Daddy?" during your reading time together. The objects in the book are organized so as to provide an understanding of the grouping or classification of objects. After a trip to the zoo, you can recall the animals your child has seen by turning to the section entitled "At the Zoo". There are over forty sections which will help your child begin to organize his everyday experiences.

ACTIVITY 1: Modeling Clay

Learning
Operation:
Acquiring the manipulative motions—squeezing, poking, rolling, pounding, rounding, pinching—appropriate to handling clay.

Materials:
Clay or play dough

Presentation:
Preparation. Provide a work surface that can be scrubbed. A Formica tabletop is excellent, but you can cover your table with a piece of oil cloth or heavy plastic. Perhaps you can get a sink cutout of a Formica countertop from a local carpenter.

Independent Discovery. Give your toddler a piece of clay and encourage him to manipulate it freely. He may enjoy it if you sit with him and pinch, poke and roll the clay, too. Do not try to make objects. The focus of this activity is to discover how many things you can do to clay, not what you can make from it.

Guided Practice. As your child plays with the clay, show him how to roll out long sausages of clay or how to make round little balls by rolling the clay in the palms of your hands or on the tabletop. He will be interested in flattening out the clay and poking it with his fingers or a fork. He may also enjoy pressing it with bottle caps or small cookie cutters. If he enjoys making round balls, let him make a snowman, but don't insist on object representation. As this developmental level, he should be enjoying the physical sensations of squeezing, poking, pounding and rolling and should be interested in how these actions affect the clay.

OBSERVING PROGRESS

Does your child experiment freely with the clay dough?

☐ yes   ☐ no

If not, continue to provide opportunities for free play and be sure that you are not giving the child too many directions. Perhaps it would be a good idea to leave him completely alone with the clay.

If yes, go on to the suggestion in the VARIATION below.

ACTIONS OR RESPONSES
I WOULD LIKE TO REMEMBER

_____

_____

_____

TEST OF MASTERY: Given play dough or clay, the child enjoys manipulating it and demonstrates skill in squeezing, rolling, pounding and pinching it.

Toddler's Age in Months at Mastery _____

VARIATION

Making Clay: You may want to provide clay dough in other colors for your youngster, but do not purchase modeling clay as this material is too stiff for a toddler to manipulate easily. He is sure to enjoy, however, making clay dough with you.

Mix together 1 part salt, 2 parts flour and 1 part water. Knead the mixture to make sure the ingredients are well blended. Divide the dough into several portions and color each with vegetable food coloring. Watching the color spread through the dough is exciting to the toddler, so do not prepare the dough without his help. If you place this dough in a plastic bag or empty plastic container and store it in the refrigerator, it will remain soft and pliable for a long time.

SUPPLEMENTARY MATERIALS
OR ACTIVITIES OF MY OWN

_____

_____

_____

_____

RECOMMENDED TOYS

Puzzle 'n' Mold - Trace 'n' Play (Child Guidance)

Small rolling pin

Cookie cutters

ACTIVITY 2: Line Drawing

Learning Operation: Acquiring the fine finger control necessary for success in scribbling and drawing lines.

Materials: Large crayons, newsprint, 18″ x 24″

Presentation: *Independent Exploration.* Provide your toddler with daily opportunities to experience the wonder of color and the fun of movement as he learns to control the direction of the crayon he chooses. Large newsprint provides a good sized area for the child's early scribbling. Freedom and experimentation are the key words in these early drawing experiences. As you place the newsprint and crayons on the table in front of your toddler, encourage him to try all of the colors. In the beginning he will and *should* scribble.

Guided Practice. **Round-and-Round Motion:** Your toddler will enjoy using his crayon to make a rhythmic *round-and-round* motion. Stand behind him and put your hand over his to take his hand through this motion. He will enjoy this activity more if you say *"round and round and round"* as you help him make repeated circular patterns on the paper. Do not make cramped circular motions involving only his fingers, but use a free swing which involves his hand and arm. Soon he will be drawing around and around on his own.

Learning to Stop: Encourage your toddler to scribble without inhibition and to make the round-and-round motion over and over again, but you can also teach him to stop at the completion of a circular motion. Stand behind and guide his hand through the round motion of one circle, saying as you do, "Round and STOP!" Pull his hand up at the completion of the circle. Make it fun, and he will enjoy learning to stop as he covers a page with many separate circles. He will still find circular scribblings fun and will continue to make his round-and-round motions, but he will be pleased with his ability to make a single circle.

Horizontal Lines: After your toddler has mastered the round-and-round motion and has sufficient control to enjoy coming to a stop, introduce horizontal lines. Draw horizontal lines across the paper, first short ones and then longer ones. Encourage him to make lines like yours. If his continue to be short, put your hand over his before he has stopped and push his crayon along to stretch out his line. He should use his whole hand and arm in the horizontal motion and not merely his fingers.

Vertical Lines: If he is successful with horizontal lines, introduce vertical lines in a similar way. Draw short vertical lines at first and then longer ones. Encourage him to draw up and down lines like yours. If his lines continue to be short, put your hand over his before he has stopped and push the crayon along to extend the line. He should use his whole hand and arm in the vertical motion and not merely his fingers.

Crossing Lines: Show him that when you draw a line across the page and one up and down, the two lines will cross each other. Encourage him to try. Since this activity requires considerable visual/motor coordination, you may want to help the child by guiding his hand to make the intersecting line. He will feel a real sense of accomplishment when he succeeds on his own to cross the two lines. He may continue to cross the horizontal line with the vertical line or he may begin to reverse this procedure. Do not insist that he cross in only one way.

The Stick Man: You will be surprised to discover that your toddler has now developed sufficient control to imitate your drawing of a large stick man. Sit beside him at the table and share a piece of newsprint. Begin by saying, "First I'll make a circle for my man's head. Now you make a circle for your man's head. Now we'll make a long line for his body. Then we'll cross that line to make his arms. Now we'll add two more lines to make his legs."

Encourage the child to add other familiar details—hair, facial features, small circles for ears, hands and feet. Praise his drawing. Perhaps you'd like to hang it in his room or above the kitchen table.

OBSERVING PROGRESS

Does the toddler show continued interest in experimenting with his crayons and large pieces of paper?

☐ yes   ☐ no

This is the only way to measure achievement in drawing at this developmental level.

If not, continue to praise his efforts and to provide guidance from time to time without pushing him. It is not important that he master the structured sequence in a rapid day-to-day progression. Your toddler need not respond to the stick man in order to enjoy experiences with crayons and paper.

If yes, let him go! If he has daily opportunities to draw, if you praise his efforts, and if he experiences reasonable success with the activities described above, your child, during his second or third year, will love to spend time "making pictures".

ACTIONS OR RESPONSES
I WOULD LIKE TO REMEMBER

_____

_____

_____

_____

_____

TEST OF MASTERY: Given crayons and large pieces of paper, the child shows continued interest in practice and experimentation. This assessment, of course, can be made only as a result of your observation over a period of months.

Toddler's Age in Months at Mastery _____

VARIATION

Drawing and Painting: Introduce other drawing and painting materials when you have time. Be sure to plan ahead so that clean-up time for certain materials does not become an irritation or a crisis. Colored chalk and felt-tipped pens help to give new color impressions. They also add interesting texture to the drawings.

Finger painting provides a chance to experiment with color and encourages freedom in motion. The recipe for making finger paint given in DEVELOPMENTAL LEVEL 15, Activity 2 (see page 98) can be used again here.

Painting with poster paint and large brushes is also fun for toddlers. Have your youngster paint in an area where spills will not cause rug or wallpaper damage. Offer only one or two colors at first and provide a separate brush for each color. Learning to use one brush for each color is a tricky operation for a toddler, but it is the only way he can avoid muddy-looking pictures.

SUPPLEMENTARY MATERIALS
OR ACTIVITIES OF MY OWN

_____

_____

_____

_____

_____

RECOMMENDED TOYS

Scribbler's Mini Board*
(Western Publishing)

*Scribbler's is a trademark of Western Publishing, Inc.

ACTIVITY 3: Cutting

Learning Operation: Acquiring the fine finger skills for snipping, fringing, making cutouts, and continuous cutting.

Materials: Blunt scissors (If your child has shown a consistent preference for using his left hand, provide him with a pair of "lefty" scissors.)

Construction paper, 8 ½″ x 11″

Presentation: *Guided Practice.* Provide your toddler with frequent opportunities to experience the fun of cutting as he learns to control the direction and movement of the scissors. When the child is first starting there is no right way for him to hold or cut with the scissors. As in drawing, freedom and experimentation are the key words in early cutting experiences. Since he may use both to manipulate the scissors at first, you may need to hold the paper so that he is able to cut it.

Sequence of Cutting Actions. After your child has shown an interest in cutting with scissors, guide him through the following cutting motions:

Snipping: Let him use both hands to cut through half-inch strips of construction paper which you hold for him. This is really a snipping action.

Cutouts: The toddler uses a snipping motion to cut pieces of any size and shape. He may be pleased if on occasion you paste these random cuttings on a piece of white construction paper. He will be proud of this "picture" and the white background gives added focus to the shapes he has cut. You can also use his "cutouts" to make an abstract mobile to hang above his bed or the kitchen table.

Continuous Cutting: Provide a guide for him to follow. Use a felt-tipped pen to draw a heavy line across a sheet of paper. Ask your toddler to cut along that line or to follow "the road" with his scissors. Begin with a small piece of paper and a short line so his hand does not tire. If he enjoys activities of this nature, introduce longer lines, curves and even zigzag lines. Some toddlers will even progress to cutting around a circle or a square, but do not make these cutting tasks too complicated.

Fringing: Have him hold a small piece of paper and make short cuts stopping before the edge of the paper. At first he may snip off the pieces rather than make a fringe, but with practice he can achieve a fringe. Later, your child will enjoy cutting a fringe around a paper feather that you have cut out for him. He may also have fun cutting a fringe around a 9″ x 12″ piece of construction paper. Cover it with plastic wrap and use it as a place mat at lunchtime.

OBSERVING PROGRESS

Does the toddler hold the paper by himself and use the scissors to snip or fringe?

☐ yes   ☐ no

If not, continue to hold the paper for him until he acquires a firm grip on the scissors. Remember to use narrow strips of paper so that he can cut through them in only one snip.

If yes, help him to repeat the snipping action more or less consecutively and to hold the paper by himself.

Does the toddler snip the paper with one continuous motion?

☐ yes   ☐ no

If not, provide more snipping practice until his hand holds the scissors firmly and does not readily tire. Cutting along heavy lines or "roads" will also help to focus his attention on repeating the actions.

If yes, encourage your child's interest in cutting by making pictures, mobiles, place mats and bookmarks with the products of his cutting practice. Provide other materials to cut as suggested in the VARIATION.

ACTIONS OR RESPONSES I WOULD LIKE TO REMEMBER

_____

_____

_____

_____

TEST OF MASTERY: Given paper and blunt scissors, the toddler demonstrates a continuous cutting action.

Toddler's Age in Months at Mastery _____

VARIATION

Cutting Games: Your child will respond with new enthusiasm to cutting activities which involve unusual materials. Let him cut colored tissue paper or pieces of gift wrapping. He will also enjoy cutting up pages from newspaper and from magazines. Wallpaper remnants or samples also provide a good cutting medium. Let the child experience the resistance he meets when he tries to cut a piece of light-weight cardboard, but do not insist that he cut for a long period on heavy materials. He will be puzzled and amused when he tries to snip pieces of fabric or a piece of cellophane or tinfoil. Cutting a piece of yarn or string is a real challenge. When his scissors are dull, give him a piece of sandpaper to snip. The sandpaper offers a new cutting texture and will sharpen the blades of his scissors as he cuts.

SUPPLEMENTARY MATERIALS OR ACTIVITIES OF MY OWN

_____

_____

_____

RECOMMENDED TOYS

The Scribbler's* Scissor Book
(Western Publishing)

*Scribbler's is a trademark of Western Publishing, Inc.

ACTIVITY 4: Pasting

Learning Operation: Acquiring the manipulative skills associated with pasting.

Materials: Wheat paste and paste brush
Scissors
Construction paper - 18″ x 24″
Tissue paper

Presentation: *Preparation.*   Add water to the wheat paste, thinning it so that it can be easily applied with a brush. If the paste is too thick, your toddler will have difficulty spreading it. Cover the work area with newspaper to avoid unnecessary clean-up chores.

Independent Practice.   As your toddler freely cuts pieces from construction paper, save his cuttings. Help him paste them on a large sheet of construction paper to make a picture. Allow him the freedom to arrange his pieces as he chooses. He may want to paste one cutting on top of another or build up several layers of cuttings. Leave him alone—he's really making a three-dimensional collage! Some youngsters prefer to paste with their fingers, so do not insist that a paste brush be used. There is only one restriction in this activity—pasting must stay on the sheet of construction paper.

Elaboration. On another day, offer the tissue paper as the medium for a similar pasting project. Your toddler may enjoy tearing off pieces of tissue rather than cutting them. The ragged edges add to the effect of his picture. Let him arrange the pieces of tissue on a large piece of construction paper and, holding the pieces in place, generously paste over the pieces to secure them. Again, he may build up several layers of tissue. As the paste is brushed over the tissue, the colors run and the visual effect is very satisfying to the youngster.

OBSERVING PROGRESS

Does the child show continuing interest in practice and experimentation with pasting activities?

☐ yes   ☐ no

If not, continue to offer opportunities to paste. Be sure that you are not expressing irritation over the mess that pasting activities produce. Have your toddler wear a smock or apron. Be sure to cover the work surface with newspaper so you don't have to scrub up later. Your child cannot become happily involved in these experiences if he senses that you will be upset if he makes a mess.

If yes, encourage him to complete other pasting projects as suggested in the VARIATIONS.

ACTIONS OR RESPONSES I WOULD LIKE TO REMEMBER

_____

_____

_____

TEST OF MASTERY: The toddler pastes small pieces of paper which he has cut or torn onto a larger piece of paper in arrangements of his own choosing.

Toddler's Age in Months at Mastery _____

VARIATIONS

Decorations: From time to time, help your toddler complete a pasting project in which he actually makes something to use or to give to another person. He can, for instance, paste several of his paper cuttings onto a brown paper bag. The bag, in turn, can be used to take cookies to a friend.

Let him decorate a gift package. Wrap the box in plain paper and let your toddler paste on his cuttings. Add a ribbon or yarn bow and you have a package sure to please another family member or friend.

Scrapbooks: Your toddler may also enjoy making a simple scrapbook of his cuttings. You need not spend money purchasing a scrapbook. Instead, fold five sheets of newsprint in half and staple on the fold. You now have a ten-page scrapbook.

A similar book can be made from large sheets of construction paper or you may punch holes in small sheets and tie them together with ribbon or yarn. Your toddler will find it satisfying to paste cuttings in this book from time to time. Do not encourage him to complete the scrapbook at one sitting unless he insists on filling all the empty pages.

SUPPLEMENTARY MATERIALS OR ACTIVITIES OF MY OWN

_____

_____

_____

_____

ACTIVITY 5: Tracing

Learning Operation: Experiencing form and boundaries with tracing frames.

Materials: 3 tracing frames: a square, a circle, a triangle

Presentation:

Preparation. Cut three, 6″ square frames out of posterboard. On each piece trace and cut out a 3″ diameter circle, a square (each side = 3″) and a triangle (each side = 3″).

Preview. Let your toddler examine the three tracing frames. Encourage him to run his index finger around the inside boundary of each shape. He should be able to identify at least one or two of these if he has been successful with the activities at DEVELOPMENTAL LEVELS 12 and 16 (see pages 73-83 and 102-111). If he cannot name a shape, name it for him. Point out that his finger goes *around* and *around* the circle but that it *bumps* into the corners of the square and the triangle.

Demonstration. Place the circle frame on a piece of newsprint and hold it firmly with one hand. Select a crayon and trace around the circle, pushing against the edge of the circle. Lift the frame and show the child the circle you have made.

Guided Tracing Practice. Give him the frame and a crayon. Stand behind him to help. You may need to guide his tracing hand until he feels the resistance offered by the edge, and you may also have to help to hold the frame securely on the paper. He will be delighted with his tracing because it is as good as yours! Continue to help him as he makes several circles.

Independent Practice. Soon your toddler will be able to hold the frame firmly with one hand and trace the circle with the other. Encourage him to change crayons and to make many circles. Then introduce the square and triangle. He may be able to handle these frames without any further help from you.

Elaboration. Your toddler will create many interesting activities with the frames. Praise his discoveries and include the following activities when he plays with the frames.

Show him how he can fully color in a shape by holding the frame securely and going back and forth inside the edges. Coloring in a shape requires time and effort. Help hold the frame if his hand slips and the frame moves. He will not be able to refit the frame over the shape without your help.

Show your child how to draw one shape outline over another by moving the frames. He may have discovered this interesting design technique all by himself.

If the child is showing interest in representing objects in his freehand drawing with crayons, he may enjoy using the frames to construct simple familiar pictures. Help him to add details to the basic shapes. Two circles make a snowman. Simple features make a circle into a face, a string makes it a balloon, a stick makes it a lollipop. A trunk makes a triangle a tree. Windows and a door make a square a house. Your child may be able to put a circle on top of the triangle to make an ice cream cone. The triangle on top of the square makes an even more elaborate house. Two triangles base-to-base make a kite when you add a string.

OBSERVING PROGRESS

Does the toddler hold the frame firmly with one hand and trace the shape with the other?

☐ yes   ☐ no

If not, continue to help him by guiding his tracing hand or by helping him to hold the frame securely against the paper. He may become so absorbed in tracing that he releases his hold on the frame, allowing it to slip and spoiling his tracing. Help him at once before he gets discouraged. He wants his circle to be perfect—just like the one he saw you make.

If yes, encourage him to play with the frames by himself. Introduce the elaborations for more structured drawings when you think he is ready.

ACTIONS OR RESPONSES I WOULD LIKE TO REMEMBER

_____

_____

_____

TEST OF MASTERY: Given a tracing frame, a crayon and paper, the toddler holds the frame securely on the paper with one hand and traces around the edges of the shape with a crayon held in the other hand.

Toddler's Age in Months at Mastery _____

VARIATION

Shape Book: Follow the suggestions for making a newsprint or construction paper scrapbook (see Activity 4, page 118) to make a shape book. Your toddler may be interested in making shapes of a different color on each page or placing several tracings on top of one another to make designs. He will enjoy showing his shape book to others, which will encourage him to use the shape words he is learning.

He can also combine his cutting skills, if they are adequate, with his tracing and pasting skills. Suggest that he cut around his shape tracings and paste them on a sheet of paper. If you provide colorful construction paper, the end product will be more satisfying. Yellow and orange cutouts, for instance, make a strong contrast when pasted on blue or black paper.

SUPPLEMENTARY MATERIALS OR ACTIVITIES OF MY OWN

_____

_____

_____

RECOMMENDED TOYS

The Scribbler's* Stencil Book
(Western Publishing)

*Scribbler's is a trademark of Western Publishing, Inc.

18

PATTERNING

When you take an object away from a group of familiar objects, your toddler will be able to tell you what is missing. His previous experiences with visual memory activities at DEVELOPMENTAL LEVELS 4 and 8 (see pages 19-23 and 45-51) and with fitting parts to form a whole at DEVELOPMENTAL LEVEL 13 (see page 84) help to ensure his success at this level. When he plays "What's Missing?" with confidence and enthusiasm, he is ready to complete more complex patterns. He will enjoy handling the teddy bear miniatures to reconstruct a color pattern you have made, matching the colors from left to right. Later, he will reproduce a simple story pattern with felt cutouts, taking his cues only from your words instead of copying your pattern. In the last activity of this level, he will put five rods of different lengths in order in a staircase pattern.

Parallel Language Development. Your child will probably be a good spontaneous talker by the time he is successful with the activities in this unit. As you read familiar stories to him—*Little Red Hen, Three Little Pigs, The Gingerbread Man*—he will be chiming in regularly, telling the part of the story he knows, especially if you ask, "And then what happens?" Be sure to provide opportunities for him to take a turn as you enjoy reading time together.

ACTIVITY 1: What's Missing?

Learning
Operation: The toddler improves his visual memory and demonstrates his readiness to reproduce more complex patterns.

Materials: Small objects, plastic container

Presentation: *Preparation.* Place an assortment of small objects with which your toddler is very familiar into the container. Choose only objects which you know he can *name*. Use small materials—several wooden blocks, beads, wooden shapes, a crayon, the scissors, a toy car, a spoon, a button, a pencil. Change the contents of the sorting tray from time to time to maintain interest in the game.

Focusing Attention. Begin by announcing, "Let's play a game. I'm taking a *block* and a *crayon* and a *button* out of this container."

Line these objects up on the table in front of your toddler and say, "Look here and tell me what you see."

After he names the objects, acknowledge his answers by saying. "That's good. You know what they are."

If there was an object he could not name, point to it and name it. Ask him to repeat that word.

The Memory Game. Now ask him to close his eyes. As he does so, quietly remove one of the objects, for example, the crayon. Then say, "Open your eyes and tell me what's missing. What did I take away?"

If he answers *crayon,* praise his observation. "How smart you are! You know what was missing. Let's play the game again."

If he cannot name the missing object, show it to him, replace it with the others, and play the game again.

Elaboration. As you continue to play, vary the objects. If your toddler is consistently successful in identifying a missing object from a field of three objects, add another item. Play this game for a few minutes each day and soon your toddler will be able to name the missing item from a field of five, six or even seven objects. Remember to change the contents of your "memory box".

OBSERVING PROGRESS

Does the toddler consistently identify the missing object from a field of three objects?

☐ yes   ☐ no

If not, review the presentation, making certain that you are using objects he can name. If he seems confused, present the game using only two objects and then add the third.

If yes, gradually increase the number of objects in the field until you reach seven.

Does the toddler consistently identify the missing objects from a field of seven?

☐ yes   ☐ no

If not, drop down to the number at which he is successful and very gradually build back up to seven. Remember, you can only use objects which he can name.

If yes, continue to play this game for brief periods daily with your toddler. Incorporate the suggestions given in the VARIATIONS.

ACTIONS OR RESPONSES I WOULD LIKE TO REMEMBER

_____

_____

_____

_____

TEST OF MASTERY: The toddler is given the opportunity to study and name a field of seven objects and then closes his eyes while one object is removed. When he reopens his eyes and re-examines the field, he names the missing object.

Toddler's Age in Months at Mastery _____

VARIATIONS

Toddler as Teacher: You will spark your toddler's interest in the memory game if you take turns being the "teacher" Let him take objects out of the memory box and line them up. You close your eyes while he secretly removes one of the objects. Make the game fun by occassionally pretending that you have difficulty "remembering" a missing object.

Two Missing Objects: If your toddler is very successful in this game, try removing two objects when he closes his eyes. Give him time to name two objects before you show him what you have done. If you decide to try this version, do not use more than five objects and do _not_ increase the number of missing objects beyond two at any point.

Memory Games: Encourage him to play simple memory games with you that concern his everyday routines. If, for instance, you put out his clothes to help him dress in the morning, make a game of it by saying, "Here are your underwear, your socks, your shirt and your pants."

Put out each item as he watches you. Then say, "What's missing?"

He probably will not respond shoes because he has not recently seen the shoes, but with repetition he will name the missing items and will enjoy playing this game immensely. If you have time, you can play other versions—dressing to go outdoors (snowsuit, cap, mittens, boots) or getting ready to eat (plate, cup, spoon, bib). Invent versions of your own, but remember that you must play each version often if your toddler is to succeed.

SUPPLEMENTARY MATERIALS OR ACTIVITIES OF MY OWN

_____

_____

_____

_____

ACTIVITY 2: Color Patterns

Learning Operation: Reconstructing a color pattern in left-to-right progression [one-to-one matching.

Materials: *Teddy Bear Counters* (Milton Bradley)

Presentation:

Preview. Let your toddler freely manipulate an assortmer of miniature teddy bears. He will delight in handling an examining them and should be encouraged to do so before yc begin the more structured portion of the presentation. If he ha been successful at DEVELOPMENTAL LEVELS 15 and 16, h should be able to name each bear by color. Ask him to do s and praise his successes.

Establishing a Pattern. Sit *beside* him at the table or wor] from a position slightly *behind* him so that the child will no have to reverse the pattern you make. If you sit across the tabl or at right angles to the child, he must reverse the pattern whic] might confuse him. Give him a bear of each color and take a se for yourself.

Work from his left to his right, saying, "*FIRST*, I stand my *rea* teddy bear on the table. *Next* comes my *blue* teddy bear. Afte] that comes my *yellow* teddy bear. *Last* is my *green* teddy bear."

Guided Patterning Practice. Say to him, "Can you line up your bears to look like mine?"

Help him to look carefully at your line of bears by asking, "Which bear comes first?"

After he places his red bear, ask, "Which bear is next?" Continue until he has completed the four-bear color pattern. Repeat this presentation only *once* daily until your toddler begins to experience easy success in reconstructing a color pattern from left to right.

In the beginning, his main interest is in freely playing with the teddy bears, so be sure to let him play with the bears on his own terms before or after each presentation.

126

Subsequent Practice.   As you repeat this game with your toddler, vary the color progression of the bears and do not restrict the pattern to red-blue-yellow-green. You must, however, insist that your toddler reproduce each pattern beginning on the left and proceeding to the right. Left-to-right progression is an important school-related skill, and even these simple skills needed to make line patterns are related to more complex patterns in reading and printing.

OBSERVING PROGRESS
Does the toddler successfully reconstruct a four-color pattern from left to right by using matching skills?

☐ yes   ☐ no

If not, continue to repeat your presentation once daily. It may help if you arrange your pattern on the table above his working area so that he builds his pattern immediately below yours. In this manner he may more easily check the one-to-one color match as he moves from the bear on the left to the one on the far right.

If yes, continue to offer new four-color patterns and begin to incorporate the suggestions in the VARIATIONS.

ACTIONS OR RESPONSES I WOULD LIKE TO REMEMBER

_____

_____

_____

TEST OF MASTERY: Given the necessary miniatures, the toddler reconstructs a four-color pattern moving from left to right, matching each piece to the corresponding pattern piece.

Toddler's Age in Months at Mastery _____

VARIATIONS

Complex Color Patterns: If your toddler is very successful with simple four-color patterns, introduce more complex patterns. He will enjoy patterns which involve alternation and repetition of color; for example, red-blue-red-blue or green-yellow-yellow-green. Double colors will also interest him: green-green-yellow-yellow-red-red. Continue, of course, to be certain that your child copies patterns from left to right.

All patterning tasks are much more difficult if you give your child an assortment of pieces to work from instead of giving him *only* the pieces needed to copy the pattern. If your toddler does very well, let him work from such an assortment rather than giving him only the pieces he will need.

Introduce other materials into the patterning exercises. The colored wooden blocks from DEVELOPMENTAL LEVEL 16 (see page 103) make a good combination with the teddy bears. A *very* simple story line will add to the fun. For example, a blue bear lives in a blue house (block), a red bear lives in a red house, and a green bear lives in a green house. The pattern can also be made by standing the blue bear *on* his blue house!

Patterning From Memory: You will enjoy experimenting with one final variation if your child has been excited about making patterns. Make a *very* simple pattern with the blocks or bears. Before you give him any blocks, ask him to look at your pattern very carefully. Now cover your pattern with a box and see if he can reproduce it from memory instead of by one-to-one matching. Help him lift the box to check to see if the patterns match. Give him several chances to try, but don't insist that he perform this task.

SUPPLEMENTARY MATERIALS OR ACTIVITIES OF MY OWN

_____

_____

_____

RECOMMENDED TOYS
Cubical Counting Blocks
(Milton Bradley or Ideal)

ACTIVITY 3: Story Patterns

Learning Operation: Reproducing visual patterns from verbal cues and developing listening skills.

Materials: Primary Cutouts—ducks, rabbits, birds, apples, stars and pears (Milton Bradley)

Two flannel squares

Presentation:

Preparation. Cut two 11″ flannel squares from flannel fabric.

Preview. Let your toddler play freely with the small felt cutouts and arrange them as he chooses on one of the flannel squares.

He will enjoy feeling them and will be interested in noting how they "stick" to the flannel. Encourage him to name as many of the cutouts as he can.

Demonstration. **The Story Pattern:** Sit down beside your toddler and get his attention as you would when you are about to tell a story. Then begin:

- "See my stars?" *Place stars on your flannel square.*
- "Under the stars is a rabbit fast asleep." *Place the rabbit below the stars.*
- "Up in the sky a bird is flying." *Place a bird in the sky above the rabbit and under the stars.*

Guided Story Pattern Practice: As your toddler looks at your story pattern, ask him, "Can you make a picture just like mine? Do you have some stars? Where will you put your stars?"

Do *not* encourage him to look at your pattern but if he needs to look at it, let him. Try to note whether your questions were used as *verbal* cues or whether he needed to rely on your pattern as a *visual* cue.

Provide frequent opportunities for story patterns. Continue to place the appropriate felt cutouts on your square as you tell your story. Keep the story line simple. You can, for example, tell the story of a duck and a rabbit taking a walk and they find an apple to eat.

Independent Practice: **Listening.** When you think your child can create a story pattern by himself (without having your model from which to copy), tell him a story and let him make a "picture" giving him hints by your statements and questions. Your youngster will delight in these little stories and his listening skills will improve.

OBSERVING PROGRESS

Does the toddler reconstruct your arrangement of felt objects and appear to follow your story with interest?

☐ yes ☐ no

If not, tell a shorter story involving fewer cutouts. Be deliberate in your placement of the cutouts, drawing his attention to their positions in relationship to the other pieces—above, behind, beside, under, on.

If yes, encourage him to arrange his cutouts by following what you say rather than by merely copying your placement of objects.

Does the toddler place his felt cutouts appropriately as he listens to your story and when he has no arrangement to copy?

☐ yes ☐ no

If not, continue to help him by providing an arrangement to copy. Gradually withdraw your help by encouraging him to place his cutout *before* you place yours. Finally, do not use cutouts yourself as you tell the story.

If yes, play the story game often and incorporate the VARIATION if your toddler's language development is adequate.

ACTIONS OR RESPONSES
I WOULD LIKE TO REMEMBER

_____

_____

_____

_____

_____

TEST OF MASTERY: Given a supply of felt cutouts and a flannel square, the toddler places the cutouts on the square in an arrangement which reflects the specifics of a simple story he is told.

Toddler's Age in Months at Mastery _____

VARIATION: Add to the opportunity for language development in this game and increase its social nature by encouraging your toddler to tell a simple story for you to pattern. Listen attentively and try hard to construct his story pattern. Don't forget to ask for his help, also. He will feel important and he needs to be creative, too.

You can also make other cutouts—a tree from green flannel, the sun from yellow flannel—to add to the content of your stories.

SUPPLEMENTARY MATERIALS
OR ACTIVITIES OF MY OWN

_____

_____

_____

_____

_____

ACTIVITY 4: The Staircase

Learning Operation: Sequencing varying lengths by size from longest to shortest.

Materials: Five rods or pencils, graduated in length
Staircase pattern

Presentation:

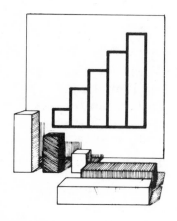

Preparation. Cut pencils or a wooden dowel into varying lengths. Make staircase pattern by tracing the lengths using a black felt-tip marker onto an 8″ square of white posterboard. Begin each line on the left side of the paper.

Preview. Let your toddler play freely with the five rods. Point out to him that they are different lengths. You may initially call them *big* and *little* or introduce the more descriptive terms of *long* and *short*. Some toddlers will recognize the difference in length between two rods if you stand them side by side on end (upright) rather than putting them flat on the table.

Demonstration: **Following the Staircase Pattern.** Introduce the patterning activity by placing the shortest rod on the shortest line. Say, "I'm going to put these rods in order. First, I put the little rod—the *shortest* rod—in this corner. Now I'm going to put down this rod; it's just a little bit *longer*. See? I'm making steps with the rods. Which rod do you think comes next?"

Let the toddler try. Help him check his choice against the pattern and to find the correct rod.

"Can you see steps now? Which rod comes next? Good! Now only one rod is left. It is the *longest* rod. Can you put it down? There! Our staircase is finished."

Independent Patterning. After you have filled in the staircase pattern with your toddler, say, "Okay, it's your turn now. Can you put the rods in order? Can you make a staircase?"

Offer help by asking him where he will start. Encourage him by praising his correct choices. Don't say "No-no" when he chooses incorrectly. Rather, point to the correct rod and say, "Let's try that one. Good! You've got the right one!" Encourage him to repeat this activity often until he can follow the staircase pattern with ease. Be sure that he begins with the shortest rod in the left-hand corner of the pattern.

OBSERVING PROGRESS

Does your toddler successfully follow the staircase pattern and place the five rods in order from the shortest to the longest?

☐ yes   ☐ no

If not, continue to help and encourage him. Let him place the first and last rods (where there is less chance for error) while you place the three middle rods. Gradually encourage him to add one of these until he is able to follow the pattern without your help.

If yes, reinforce his patterning skill by encouraging him to use the appropriate words to describe the rods—*short (-er, -est)* and *long (-er, -est).* Remember that these terms will depend on the specific operation. A rod may be shorter than the rod to the right but longer than the rod to the left. Be tolerant as your toddler attempts to describe what he sees and does. He may describe his operations using only the words *long* and *short* and still manage to communicate a fair amount of information. When he is successful in copying the staircase pattern, go to the VARIATIONS.

ACTIONS OR RESPONSES I WOULD LIKE TO REMEMBER

_____

_____

_____

TEST OF MASTERY: Given five rods, each different length, and a staircase pattern matching the lengths of the rods, the toddler places the rods in order on the pattern from the shortest to the longest rod.

Toddler's Age in Months at Mastery _____

VARIATIONS

Other Staircases: If your toddler can copy the staircase pattern without difficulty, encourage him to reproduce it without the pattern. He will need a guide to keep the base ends of the rods even, so paste a strip of adhesive or colored transparent tape on the tabletop to serve this purpose. Again, he will probably be able to supply the end rods without difficulty but may need help with the middle three.

Up and Down the Staircase: When you have completed a vertical staircase, encourage your toddler to "walk up" the staircase with his fingers. Feeling the equal steps as well as seeing them will help him to conceptualize the size relationships. He will also enjoy taking one of the teddy bear miniatures (Activity 2, page 126) and helping the bear climb the stairs. You can accentuate the ascending staircase by repeating, "up, up, up, up, up," as the teddy bear climbs and "down, down, down, down, down" as it descends the staircase.

Measuring Games: Be alert for everyday opportunities which can intensify his understanding of long and short and his interest in patterning according to length. He may find new pleasure in climbing the staircase at home after he has been working with the staircase pattern. He will enjoy "measuring" his shoelace with one from your shoes. He can compare the lengths of three or four shoes or socks and arrange them in order.

A walk to the park can provide an occasion to find sticks of different lengths. These can be examined in the park and laid out in order. He can make a long and a short road in the sandbox for his toy cars. Chalk lines are fun to draw on the sidewalk, and a long one might extend all the way across the lot!

SUPPLEMENTARY MATERIALS OR ACTIVITIES OF MY OWN

_____

_____

_____

RECOMMENDED TOYS

Color Peg Board (Brio)

EARLY CLASSIFICATION

Your toddler now begins to identify an object according to the characteristics which make it part of a group of objects. He will enjoy the first activity as he learns to group familiar objects by their use—things to play with and things to wear. Later, he learns to identify the general characteristics which enable us to classify animals, buildings, trees, people and vehicles. Classifying or grouping wooden miniatures is only the beginning of the classification games he can play.

Parallel Language Development. Extend your child's understanding of classification by engaging him in daily conversations about likenesses and differences. At mealtime, talk about the differences between fruits and vegetables, which animals supply milk, meat, and eggs, and how we make bread. See if he remembers the story of the *Little Red Hen* and how she made bread. On walks, talk about things that grow in the ground—the trees, grass, and flowers. Ask him which we pick and use to make our house look pretty. Encouraging him to ask questions about his daily experiences is an important step in extending his understanding and use of language.

ACTIVITY 1: Things to Play With; Things to Wear

Learning Operation: Classifying objects according to function.

Materials: Assortment of materials - toys and clothing
Sorting tray

Presentation: *Preparation.* Put a collection of small toys into the sorting tray. Include items used in earlier presentations—several beads on a lace, the threading block, a wooden block, a teddy bear miniature (as well as other small toys: a car, a doll, a ball, a stuffed animal). Add small items of clothing: your child's shoe, a sock, a slipper, a mitten, a glove, a scarf, a cap, earmuffs, an old necktie, perhaps an undershirt or jersey.

Demonstration. **Establishing Two Classes:** Sit on the floor with your toddler and put the sorting tray beside you. Pull out the sock and ask him what you do with it. He will probably indicate that it belongs on his foot. Add to his observation:

"Yes, you *wear* a sock on your foot. A sock is *something to wear.*"

Put the sock on the floor, saying, "Things to wear will go on this pile."

Now pull out the toy car. "What do you do with this?" The child will probably indicate that he pushes it on the floor. Again, expand on his response, "Yes, you *play* with a toy car. A toy car is *something to play with.*"

Put the car on the floor about three feet from the sock and say, "Things to play with will go on this pile."

Guided Classification Practice. Now let the child choose an item from the sorting tray and continue to follow the presentation outlined above. Each item must be classified as *something to wear* or *something to play with* and placed in the appropriate pile. Encourage your youngster to examine these objects before making a decision. Let him model the necktie or the scarf so its function is clear to him. Ask him to demonstrate how he plays with a toy—a ball is bounced, the dolly is hugged.

After you have helped him to classify five or six items, see if he is able to classify the remaining items. Continue, however, to supply a verbal description of why the object is with the group *after* he has made his classification decision.

By the way, if you have included a string of wooden beads, recognize that your toddler may correctly classify that item as either "something to wear" or "something to play with."

OBSERVING PROGRESS

Does the toddler indicate that he understands that, based on its function, he is putting items of clothing (something to wear) in one pile and toys (something to play with) in the other?

☐ yes   ☐ no

If not, help him to demonstrate the use of each object by trying on the items of clothing and by showing how he plays with the toys.

If yes, encourage him to classify as many of these items as he can without help from you. If he thought the game was fun, he may want to play it again.

ACTIONS OR RESPONSES I WOULD LIKE TO REMEMBER

_____

_____

_____

_____

_____

TEST OF MASTERY: Given a collection of small toys and items of clothing, the toddler classifies them by putting the things to wear in one pile and the things to play with in another. He is not expected to establish and define the two classes without adult help, but he is expected to sort at least three items in each class correctly without assistance.

Toddler's Age in Months at Mastery _____

SUPPLEMENTARY MATERIALS OR ACTIVITIES OF MY OWN

_____

_____

_____

_____

_____

ACTIVITY 2: Familiar Objects in the Neighborhood

Learning Operation: Classifying by classes: animals, buildings, trees, people, and vehicles.

Materials: *Wooden Toys By The Half Pound* (Constructive Playthings)
5 sorting cups (margarine containers)

Presentation: *Preview.* Let your toddler play freely with the assortment of wooden miniatures and arrange them as he chooses on the table. As he plays, familiarize the child with the names of the first two classes you will present: *buildings* and *animals*. Ask him to show you a building and an animal. Elaborate by pointing out and naming all of the miniatures which are buildings and all of those which are animals.

Guided Practice: **Establishing Two Classes.** Put three sorting cups on the table and ask your toddler if he can put *all of the animals* in one cup and *all of the buildings* in another. In the third he should put whatever he has left over. If he hesitates, drop an animal miniature in one container, saying, "The *animals* go in this cup. What goes in the other cup?"

If he hesitates again, drop a building miniature into that container, saying, "The *buildings* go in that cup." He should now be able to continue the operation.

Extending the Classification Operation. When you are satisfied that your toddler knows that horses, cows, and so on, make up the animal class and such items as houses and churches comprise the building class, add another cup and a new class: trees (things that grow). On following days continue the activity, adding the remaining classes of *vehicles and people*. Provide opportunities for practice until your toddler can easily place the wooden miniatures in the five classes.

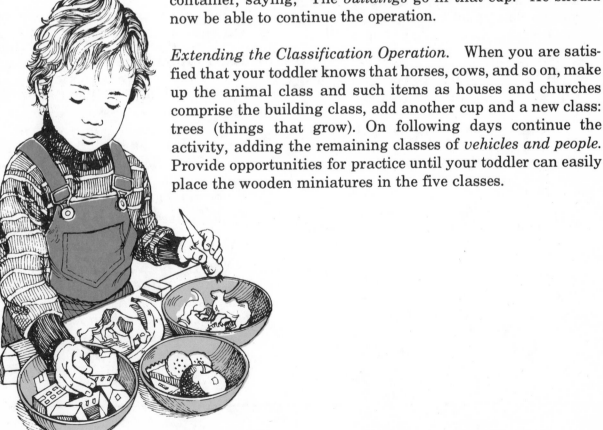

Reinforcing the Operation. Help your toddler to understand these five classes more fully by playing the classifying games when he accompanies you on neighborhood errands. Help him, for instance, to watch for all the animals—dogs, birds, squirrels, cats—as you take a walk. Emphasize the animals' names but also repeat the class: "Yes, that is a dog. A dog is also an animal."

Trees can be an interesting class if you take time to point out little trees and big trees or perhaps a tree in bloom or one without leaves. He can feel the needles on a pine tree and will enjoy being

OBSERVING PROGRESS

Does the toddler successfully classify the animal and the building miniatures into two classes?

☐ yes ☐ no

If not, continue to name the miniatures as your toddler plays with them on his own terms. Repeat the class names: buildings and animals, and observe again that houses and churches (pointing to the appropriate miniatures) are buildings and horses and cows (pointing to the appropriate miniatures) are animals. Introduce the classification activity again.

If yes, gradually incorporate the remaining three classes into the operation. Be sure to repeat these class names often as he plays with the miniatures.

Does the toddler successfully classify the wooden miniatures into five classes?

☐ yes ☐ no

If not, use fewer classes and gradually reintroduce the others. Do not be in a hurry to complete the series.

If yes, continue to play the classifying game and include the VARIATIONS.

ACTIONS OR RESPONSES I WOULD LIKE TO REMEMBER

_____

_____

_____

_____

_____

TEST OF MASTERY: Given a collection of wooden miniatures and five sorting cups, the child classifies the miniatures according to five classes: animals, buildings, trees, people and vehicles. It is acceptable for an adult to help him define these categories by naming them, but the child should place the materials in the appropriate groups by himself.

Toddler's Age in Months at Mastery _____

VARIATIONS

Adding New Classes: While walking through the neighborhood, identify "things that go": bicycles, motorcycles, cars, trucks, buses, trains.

The picture sorting game you made with gummed seals in DEVELOPMENTAL

ifted up high to touch the leaves on a very tall tree. How different trees can be, but they all belong to the same class. Buildings are also fun for him to classify: his house and the neighbor's house, an apartment house, the grocery store, the gas station, a motel, a church. Even a doghouse or a birdhouse might be included in this case. In the house, help him to classify "things to eat" as food: bread, milk, fruits, vegetables, meat, and so on. Do not, of course, attempt more than one or two classes at a time.

LEVEL 16, Activity 4 (page 110) may be used in a new way at this level. Combine, for instance, a variety of flower cards and a variety of bird cards. Your toddler may now sort these into separate containers as a classifying activity. Add new classes later—fish, farm animals or fruit.

Collecting Pictures: Other classifying games with more variety and even greater learning potential may be made by cutting small pictures from catalogs and magazines and pasting them on 4″ squares of cardboard. Classes your toddler will enjoy include vehicles, toys, clothing, furniture and foods. In addition to classifying experiences, these activities provide an excellent opportunity to add to his storehouse of names and labels (nouns).

Making Books: If your toddler enjoyed making home-made scrapbooks for pasting projects a DEVELOPMENTAL LEVEL 17 (page 120), he may want to make classification books. Prepare the booklets in advance and precut the pictures from magazines—five or six pictures for each class you want to include. After your toddler classifies the pictures, help him paste each class into a separate book-

let. He may enjoy making an animal book, a food book, a flower book, a vehicle book and, especially, a baby book. Do not, of course, attempt to complete all of these as one activity.

This is only the beginning of the classification games your toddler can play. As he get older, he may enjoy playing the games from Evelyn Sharp's book, *Thinking is Children's Play*. This book contains many interesting classification games for children three to five years old. Her book is available in a paperback edition at $1.45 from Avon Books, New York.

SUPPLEMENTARY MATERIALS OR ACTIVITIES OF MY OWN

_____

_____

_____

RECOMMENDED TOYS

Bagged Zoo Animals (Larco)

Bagged Farm Animals (Larco)

Puzzle 'n' Mold - Trace 'n' Play (Child Guidance)

Toddler Developmental Level

EARLY NUMBER CONCEPT: ONE AND MORE THAN ONE

Your toddler is introduced to the concept of *one* and *more than one* by grouping small materials and applying verbal labels. He learns to answer the important number question, *"How many?"* through the several variations which reinforce and extend his experience with the concept of numbers.

Parallel Language Development. Counting by rote from 1-10 or singing any one of the many counting songs and rhymes are easy memory feats that can be accomplished by most two-year-olds. Understanding number concepts, however, requires concrete experience in manipulating materials and one-to-one counting.

ACTIVITY 1: Grouping Objects

Learning Operation: Mastering the concept of one and more than one object and using the appropriate verbal labels.

Materials: Teddy bear miniatures—from DEVELOPMENTAL LEVEL 18 (page 126)
Sorting cup (margarine container)
2 learning mats (8 ½″ x 11″ sheets of white paper)

Presentation: *Guided Practice:* **Sets of One and More Than One.** Sit with your toddler at a low table. Bring with you the cup with the teddy bear miniatures and the two learning mats. Place one mat on the table to focus the child's attention and then place one teddy bear on it, saying, "Look! Here is *one* teddy bear."

Encourage your child to say *one bear.* Introduce the number question by asking, "How many bears do you see on the paper? Yes, one bear." Maintain his interest by your enthusiasm.

Place the second learning mat on the table and place a *handful* of teddy bears on it. Make no attempt to count these, but say, "Here is *more than one* teddy bear."

Ask him several times to point to *one* teddy bear and to point to *more than one* teddy bear.

If he can point to the correct display, use the number question "How many?" so that he must respond verbally. Point to the learning mat which contains one bear and ask the question, "How many teddy bears are here?"

Then point to the mat which contains more than one and repeat the question. If he cannot say *more than one,* supply the answer for him. Remember to repeat the number questions often as you play this game and its later variations.

Do not keep your toddler at this game for more than a few minutes. He will learn by doing the activity many times, not by the length of time he plays.

Physical Reinforcement. Now play an active number game with him which you both will enjoy and which will provide excellent reinforcement for the concept of one and more than one. Choose any physical action which your toddler enjoys—clapping, for instance. Give *one* sharp clap with your hands and say, "Here is *one* clap."

Then say, "This is *more than one* clap." Proceed to clap many times.

Your toddler will enjoy alternating between one and more than one, but remember to use the appropriate phrases to describe his actions and

OBSERVING PROGRESS

Does the toddler accurately distinguish between one and more than one teddy bear by pointing?

☐ yes ☐ no

If not, continue to play the teddy bear game for a few minutes daily. Remember to use the learning mats to focus the toddler's attention. Most important of all, continue to play the action game every day.

If yes, continue to play both games—the teddy bear game and the action game—but emphasize the child's verbal participation in the game.

Does the toddler accurately distinguish between one and more than one by giving the correct *verbal response* when asked the number questions?

☐ yes ☐ no

If not, continue to praise him when he says *one* and he will be more inclined to say *more than one*. Provide other opportunities during the day to use these words, one cup, one spoon, one shoe, and of course, more than one. Go on to the suggestions given in the VARIATIONS.

ACTIONS OR RESPONSES I WOULD LIKE TO REMEMBER

_____

_____

_____

_____

_____

TEST OF MASTERY: When asked to distinguish between displays of one and more than one object, the toddler correctly does so by pointing. He also provides the answers *one* or *more than one* when asked the number question, "How many?"

Toddler's Age in Months at Mastery _____

VARIATIONS

Grouping Games: Make sets with the other small manipulatives introduced in previous activities to vary your presentations. Colored wooden blocks and assorted shapes are fun to work with. As you repeat this activity, change the number of objects in the *more than one* display. At times put out a dozen or more objects, but at other times, put out only eight or five or three or even two. Do *not* ask your toddler to count these objects. You are merely demonstrating that groups of more than one can *look* very different but continue to be *more than one.*

Mixed Assortments: When he is *very* skillful, use a mixed assortment of objects in the presentation so that your youngster does not make the mistake of thinking that groups of more than one always contain identical items. Put out, for example, one circle shape on one mat to encourage him to do so also. Be sure to include the number question, "How many claps is this?"

Play this simple action game briefly, but often, on following days. Vary the actions: one jump and more than one jump, one tap of the foot and more than one tap, one blink of the eyes and more than one blink, one wave of the hand and more than one wave, one kiss and more than one kiss.

and an assortment of shapes on the other mat. Put out one wooden block on one mat and an assortment of objects—a block, several teddy bears, a few beads—on the other mat. You will now have to use more general terms in your questioning—one toy and more than one toy or one thing and more than one thing.

Familiar Groups: Your toddler will also think it's fun to play this game with ordinary household items—buttons, dried beans and cereals. Play the game spontaneously when your toddler is dressing or bathing—one toe and more than one toe, one finger and more than one finger. Play it as you set the table or dry the dishes—occasionally with food items—one raisin and more than one raisin, one animal cracker and more than one animal cracker. He will find it amusing to put one pea on his spoon—obviously there is more than one left on his plate.

How Many? You can make a game which you and your toddler will enjoy by cutting from catalogs and magazines pictures which illustrate the concept of *one* and *more than one*. Mount these pictures on pieces of cardboard or construction paper, all the same size. Do *not* look for identical pictures in this case but for pictures of the same *kind* of object; that is, a picture of one car and a picture of several cars. A set of eight to ten pairs is adequate. Choose subjects which appeal to your child and include some which he can name. Cup, dog, cat, tree, house are good subjects for picture pairs but he will also enjoy flower, toy, bed and chair. Play this game on the floor where you have room to spread out the pictures. Do not play with more than four or five pairs at a time, and vary the assortment you use as you repeat the game. Be sure to include the number questions: "How many?"

Two's and Three's: If your toddler has done very well with the concept of one and more than one, you may want to go on and introduce the concept of two and three in a similar way. Do this *only* if your child was very interested in games of one and more than one.

SUPPLEMENTARY MATERIALS OR ACTIVITIES OF MY OWN

_____

_____

_____

_____

_____

RECOMMENDED TOYS

Counting Cube (Child Guidance)

One Dozen Eggs (Child Guidance)

Double Six Color-Dot Dominoes (Western Publishing)

DEVELOPMENTAL

| | 0 | 3 | 6 | 9 | 12 | 15 | 18 | 21 | 24 | 27 | 3 |

INFANT

Developmental Level 1
Mouthing

Developmental Level 2
Visual Attention

Developmental Level 3
Early Eye/Hand Coordination

Developmental Level 4
Early Cognition: Interests in Objects

Developmental Level 5
Simple Motor Skills

Developmental Level 6
Letting Go

Developmental Level 7
Socialization & Imitative Behavior

Developmental Level 8
Refining Target Experiences

Developmental Level 9
Taking Apart

Developmental Level 10
Putting Together

TODDLER

Developmental Level 11
Stringing And Lacing

Developmental Level 12
Fitting Whole Shapes

Developmental Level 13
Fitting Parts To Form A Whole

Developmental Level 14
Seriation

Developmental Level 15
Matching

Developmental Level 16
Sorting

Developmental Level 17
Fine Motor Control

Developmental Level 18
Patterning

Developmental Level 19
Early Classification

Developmental Level 20
**Early Number Concepts:
One And More Than One**

The solid color indicates the point of introduction and period of active interest and mastery. The lighter shades represent children's continued interests.

Children develop at different rates and the learning pattern of individual youngsters may vary from that represented on the chart.

PROFILE CHART

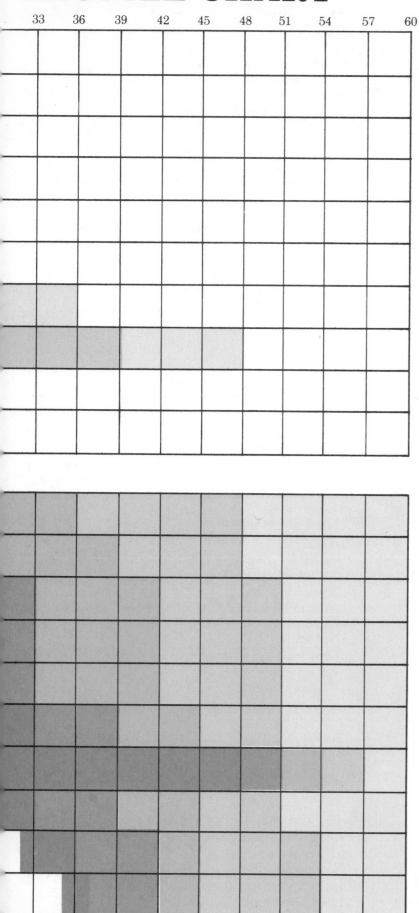

Mastery	Active Interest	Waning Interest

Appendix II: Toy Manufacturers and Suppliers

AMBI TOYS
Amsterdam, Holland

BABY WORLD, INC.
Station Plaza East
Great Neck, NY 11021

BRIO SCANDITOY AB OF SWEDEN
6531 North Sidney Place
Milwaukee, WI 53209

CHILDCRAFT EDUCATIONAL CORP.
(Catalog)
20 Kilmer Rd.
Edison, NY 08817

CHILD GUIDANCE
Gabriel Industries
Division of CBS Inc.
41 Madison Ave.
New York, NY 10010

CONSTRUCTIVE PLAYTHINGS
(Catalog)
2008 W. 1003 Terrace
Leawood, KS 66206

DENNISON MANUFACTURING CO.
Framingham, MA 01701

EDU-CARDS
P.O. Box 431
Easton, PA 18042

ENTEX INDUSTRIES
303 W. Artesia Blvd.
Compton, CA 90220

FISCHERFORM
Fischer America Inc.
14 Madison Rd.
Fairfield, NJ 07006

FISHER-PRICE TOYS
636 Girard Ave.
East Aurora, NY 14052

GALT TOYS
Box 230
63 Whitefield St.
Guilford, CT 06437

GARRARD PUBLISHING CO.
Champaign, IL 61820

HALLMARK CARDS INC.
25th & McGee Sts.
Kansas City, MO 64108

IDEAL TOY CORPORATION
200 Fifth Ave., 11th Floor
New York, NY 10010

JAMES INDUSTRIES
Hollidaysburg, PA 16648

JOHNSON & JOHNSON
501 George St.
New Brunswick, NJ 08903

JUDY COMPANY
Silver Burdett Corporation
310 N. Second St.
Minneapolis, MN 55401

KENNER PRODUCTS COMPANY
1014 Vine St.
Cincinnati, OH 45202

KIDDICRAFT
Hestair Kiddiecraft, Limited
Redlands, Ullswater Cresent
Coulsdon, Surry, England CR3 2HR

LAKESHORE CURRICULUM MATERIALS
(Catalog)
2695 E. Domingues St.
Carson, CA 90749

LAKESIDE TOYS
4400 W. 78th St.
Minneapolis, MN 55435

LAURI, INC.
Phillips
Avon, ME 04966

LEGO SYSTEMS, INC.
555 Taylor Rd.
Enfield, CT 06082

MATTEL TOYS
5150 Rosecrans
Hawthorne, CA 90250

MILTON BRADLEY CO.
1500 Main St.
Springfield, MA 01115

PLAKIE, INC.
Box 3386
Youngstown, OH 44512

PLAYSKOOL, INC.
A Milton Bradley Co.
4501 W. Augusta Blvd.
Chicago, IL 60651

SANDBERG MANUFACTURING CO.
1959 W. Fulton St.
Chicago, IL 60612

SANITOY, INC.
P.O. Box 1563
140 Sylvan Ave.
Englewood Cliffs, NY 07632

STAHLWOOD TOY MANUFACTURING CO., INC.
601 West 50th St.
New York, NY 10019

TONKA TOYS
Division of Tonka Corporation
5300 Shoreline Blvd.
Mound, MN 55364

WESTERN PUBLISHING CO., INC.
1220 Mound Ave.
Racine, WI 53404